I0477266

JOURNEYS OF THE
SALESMAN SHIP

JOURNEYS OF THE SALESMAN SHIP

Dale Dahlin

Copyright © 2011 by Dale Dahlin.

Library of Congress Control Number:		2011908819
ISBN:	Hardcover	978-1-4628-7648-8
	Softcover	978-1-4628-7636-5
	Ebook	978-1-4628-7649-5

All rights reserved. No part of this book may be reproduced or transmitted
in any form or by any means, electronic or mechanical, including photocopying,
recording, or by any information storage and retrieval system,
without permission in writing from the copyright owner.

This book was printed in the United States of America.

To order additional copies of this book, contact:
Xlibris Corporation
1-888-795-4274
www.Xlibris.com
Orders@Xlibris.com
95583

CONTENTS

The Birth of a Showman

I always wanted to be a shy kid, growing up. I was just never given the opportunity. I envied the kid down the street, who was an only child. He was never cast on the stage of life and have to live up to, or down to, the expectations of siblings and their friends. I had an elder brother and sister to contend with. My sister's friends, six years older than me, were fully developed beauty queens when I was in the embarrassing throws of puberty. When my sister invited them to our house, they would always seek me out to see how much they could make me blush by pinching my cheeks and tickling me. I think I'd rather enjoy that today, but then it was torture. It always seemed when her girlfriends were over, my brother's friends would show up. When the girls were through with me, my brother's friends would take turns, using me as a punching bag.

I guess it was then I discovered the value of "showmanship." I learned when you had someone's attention already, you could alter their designs on you by entertaining them rather than resisting them. I became so adept at this, I was able to make the bully, I had to pass on the way to school, laugh so much that he would forget to take my lunch money. Sometimes he'd just call me over to him and his friends to give them a laugh. "Make that funny face," or "play 'Yankee Doodle' with your armpit," he'd say.

I began honing my skill enough where I could evoke laughs from my teachers and coaches. Sometimes I could get an extra day or two on a late homework assignment by telling the teacher a joke about the janitor and the principal, who switched jobs for a week and no one noticed a difference except the trash cans got full. Or, I might get out of running a few laps from the PE coach by stuffing a couple footballs up my shirt and another couple down the back of my shorts and acted like the girl's coach doing jumping jacks. Of course, when she stopped me during the next gym class and said she saw my imitation, I'd get out of trouble by shoving a basketball up my shirt and act like the boy's coach, trying to attempt a pushup. I used to stretch out a lot of gym clothes.

My high school included grades 7 through 12, and by the time I was a freshman, I pretty much had the rule of the roost, or so I thought. My sister had graduated and gone off to college and my brother was a senior. His friends quit beating me up because when you became a senior, it was "uncool" to associate with an underclassman in any way. I found out there were always exceptions to rules like that in the cafeteria one day.

The 7th and 8th graders were housed mostly in one building and had the first lunch shift in the cafeteria. The second shift included grades 9 through 12. When one became a freshman, it was a big adjustment to eat with the "big kids." It was the first week of school and I was a freshman. Being with so many older kids, some actually becoming men and women, was somewhat intimidating. Most of the freshmen witnessed the demeaning tactics of the upperclassmen when one of us would innocently choose to sit at a table by the windows. Very soon they would be escorted by one of the big kids via their collar or ear to the "children's table" next to the trash cans.

It was Friday and I decided that I'd seen enough of the upperclassmen bullying the freshmen. I exited the cafeteria serving line and strode right past our crowded designated tables and took a seat at an empty table by the windows, where the seniors usually sat. I turned to look at my fellow classmates, who all had astonished looks on their faces, smiled broadly at them and turned back to my lunch tray. I had just finished opening my milk carton when I felt a hand slide down my lower back, grab my belt, and lift me out of the chair. Hanging two feet above the tray, I looked up to see the grinning face of Tommy Beatman.

Tommy was a senior and friends with my brother. Although he and the other "Beatman boys" had a great sense of humor, they also had a well-earned reputation for being tough guys. They seemed to love getting in trouble and were fearless in fights. "C'mon, Baby Dahlin," he said while laughing. "You've wandered away from the other children."

He picked up my tray in the other hand and carried me and it to an empty spot at "our" table and gently set us down.

Still laughing, he said, "Now drink all your milk, and you'll grow up to be big and strong," and he walked away.

I should have left well enough alone. I challenged the system and had won some respect from my peers. But the showman in me wasn't going to let an audience like this go to waste. I took a big swig from the milk carton and jumped up, walking after him, over-imitating his manly walk while making "he-man" poses as I went. The other kids thought this was daringly hilarious and began to laugh. I turned my head to give them my biggest stage smile while relishing in the attention. Unfortunately, I kept walking and ran right into Tommy who had stopped and turned around. The laughter fell to silence. I swung my head back and slowly looked up to Tommy's beaming smile.

"So, you think you're funny," he said. "I think you're funny, too. You know what's really funny?" He turned me sideways and wrapped one of his muscular arms around my chest. He leaned over and took the other arm and wrapped it around my legs, below the knees. Picking me up, he folded my legs back so that my heels were pressed tightly against my butt. He carried me a few feet to one of the tall, metal trash cans and stuffed me down in it, knees first. He backed up a couple feet and studied me for a moment.

"You know," he went on, "if your brother wasn't my friend, I'd stick ya in there head first." He shot an intimidating smile to the others and said, "He's funny, isn't he?" Everyone in the cafeteria, now drawn into the spectacle, nodded in agreement, even the teachers. He raised his arms above his head and shouted, "Then laugh!"

An uproariously laughter boomed through the cafeteria. Instead of crying, which is what I felt like doing, the showman in me took control and laughed along with the rest while bowing, as if it were a prearranged skit.

Tommy turned and started for the door as the laughter died down. But he stopped short and turned to face the congregation. Raising a hand he pointed to the entire crowd with a sweeping arc. Still smiling, he announced, "And if anyone helps him out," his smile vanished and was replaced with a threatening scowl, "they'll have to answer to me." And he turned and left.

The room was silent again. Slowly, the normal buzz of the cafeteria returned as I remained immobile, protruding from my trash can prison. No one spoke to me. Some would smile at me as they dumped their trash in the cans around me, but no one came to my aid, not even the teachers. I kept up the act by saying things like, "have a nice day," or "hey, you forgot your books," or "yeah, the meatloaf didn't look very good to me either."

Gradually the room cleared as the tardy bell for the next class neared. When it rang, there was no one left except for Jumbo, our huge janitor, and me. Jumbo leaned his big push broom against the wall and walked over to me.

"Help me out, Jumbo!" I pleaded.

He sized up the situation and said, "I'd like to. But I don't want to get mixed up with those Beatman boys. But I will move the other cans out of the way so you can tip yourself over and push your way out."

When I got to my next class, late of course, the teacher didn't mark me tardy and just motioned me to take my seat. As I walked to it, the other kids snickered while pointing to the ketchup and gravy stains on the knees of my pants. I just smiled and gave them a deep bow before I sat down. And the class resumed.

I don't think this episode in my life had any diminishing effect on the performer in me. Instead, I think it brought out the most becoming attribute of a true showman . . . humility.

Taking of the Mr. Softie 1-2-3

This story is dedicated to all of those sales reps and clerks whose, let's say, "salesmanship" is severely lacking in the spirit of making the customer feel appreciated for their patronage. Okay, I'm referring to the really nasty ones. You know, the ones who try to belittle you, the customer, with their condescending tone, snide remarks, and bullying attitude. The clerks at the post office come to mind, or the auto dealership parts department, or maybe even the old curmudgeon or young punk working your sales counter right now. It's rare when a poorly treated customer has the nerve or takes the time to confront the overbearing "sales person." But when they do and it's brought to the attention of management, swift and corrective action should be taken. When it is, painful as it may be, the results are often heartwarming and profitable. When it isn't, the customer simply goes away forever. If you are one of these "sales types," beware. Your correction may take you by surprise.

"And I said it was a strike!" Fatty repeated as he spit in his catcher's mitt and then rubbed a handful of dusty home plate dirt in it.

"C'mon, play ball," echoed through the players in the field. Some of them lost interest in the game and started chasing grasshoppers in the ankle-high grass.

"You wouldn't know a strike if it bit you on your big, fat butt!" rebuffed Eric, the batter, who was one of the bigger kids on the block.

"Oh yeah, sting bean?" shot back Fatty, still crouching.

"Yeah, you tub-o-lard!" Eric challenged back.

Fatty scooped up a handful of dirt and threw it on Eric's feet. The batter retaliated and kicked a pile of dirt on the catcher's worn-out chest protector. The two leaped at each other, and the first skirmish of our late summer afternoon ball game began.

"Crimany," said Merrill in disgust as he threw his glove on the ground and stormed off the miniature pitcher's mound heading for home plate. Most of the other kids instantly formed a circle around the two wrestling in the dirt while some of the others preferred to join in the grasshopper catching contest in the outfield. The shouting spectators, cheering for their particular teammate, raised the attention of "the girls" who were playing Hopscotch on the sidewalk between home plate and the street. Seeing it was just another "boy's thing" they resumed their play except for Janie, Eric's little sister. Picking up a piece of fist-sized chalk from the sidewalk she ran to the aid of her big brother.

Edging her way into the circle she started yelling, "Get 'em Eric. Get Fatty!" and she threw the chalk at Fatty as they held each other in a headlock in the dirt. Her throw missed wildly over them but found its target right in the middle of Benny's forehead, who was watching from the other side. Grabbing his face he fell to the ground, shrieking, "I'm blind, I'm blind!" It was just another repeat of yesterday's game, same as the day before that, and so on.

Typically, all of the neighborhood kids were there that day. That is except for Pete, who at age thirteen was the oldest and biggest and had just gotten a part-time job at the grocery store. Pete was our leader and peacemaker who refereed our spats and always acted as a safe haven for the underdog in an uneven battle.

Today's match had reached a stalemate and Benny was sitting up, rubbing the bump on his forehead, when everyone heard the sweet siren's song of the ice-cream truck coming down the street.

Merrill leaned over the grunting twosome and shouted, "Time out!"

Both dutifully released each other and stood up, dusting themselves off. Janie walked through the center of the circle, patted her brother on the back, and went to the aid of Benny.

"You okay?" she said, pulling his arm in an effort to help him up.

We may have had our differences, but we were a tight-knit group of kids who had our own set of rules and could be trusted to stand up for each other when the chips were down.

Throughout the summer the "Mr. Softie" ice-cream truck had always garnered our attention, and the moment we heard the familiar jingle from its roof-mounted speaker, we came running. By the time the truck stopped at the corner, it was surrounded by twenty or so kids, clutching on to their nickels, dimes, and quarters. As everyone was served we would take our places, sitting on the curb, enjoying our favorite treats of ice-cream sandwiches and cones, fudge sickles, bomb pops, and frozen malt cups.

Each year we would have a different Mr. Softie salesman/driver. They were usually jovial, older gentlemen who liked to sing and whistle a lot. They were always glad to see us, and if one of the little girls forgot her money, it wasn't unusual for the man to give her a sherbet push-pop, pat her on the head, and tell her she could repay him the next day. When she did, it would make him laugh and sing all the merrier. It would have made for a classic Norman Rockwell picture.

This year, things were different. The cheery salesman had been replaced with a coarse individual in his twenties. He didn't talk much and never smiled. He was rarely on time and some days didn't show up at all. As the summer drew on, his disposition grew worse, and he would snarl at the children if they took too long making up their minds. The unforgivable instance occurred on the same day as Eric's and Fatty's scrap, when little Melissa was the last child to be served.

She handed the salesman a fifty-cent piece and said proudly, "I got that from the tooth fairy this morning," and she smiled a tooth-missing grin to prove it.

"So what do you want, kid?" he grumbled, while slipping the coin in his pocket.

"I'd like an ice-cream sandwich," she proclaimed, nodding her head with each word.

"That's great kid, but they cost a quarter and you only gave me a nickel," he said harshly, looking around to see that no one else was there. "Here's a push-pop," shoving the small treat in her tiny hands. "Now keep your yap shut," he said, slamming the window closed and then driving away.

Heartbroken, Melissa toddled over to the others on the curb and just stood there with big crocodile tears rolling down her face.

"What's the matter, sweetie?" said Jill, the oldest of the girls, who mothered over them all.

After hearing her sobbed story, she stood up and said, "Here, honey, you can have the rest of my ice-cream bar. Let's go tell what happened to your mom."

Pete, riding his bicycle home from work, met the two on their way to Melissa's house. After finishing the troubling story, Jill gently tapped on Pete's chest with her finger and said, "You need to do something about that guy." The two were sweet on each other, and Pete nodded, acknowledging he got the message. He rode on and joined the rest of the group still convened at the corner.

"Okay," he said with authority, "it's time for us to straighten out Mr. Softie. This is what we're gonna do." They huddled in a circle, and Pete took the chalk from Benny's one hand while he was holding a malt cup to the knot on his head with the other. While drawing diagrams on the pavement, he issued the various orders:

"First, Merrill and Eric, you guys . . ."

"Second, Donald and me will . . ."

"Third, that's when Fatty, Dale, and the others . . ." and the plan was set.

The next day started differently than the carbon-copy others. We went to the bicycle shop to get the biggest inner tube and patches we could buy. Then to the office supply store to get their largest rubber bands, and finally to the small orchard that was next to our ball field. After fashioning our attack weapons to our liking and a brief rehearsal, we settled down for a game of ball.

None of us knew, or even cared, what the score was as our minds were preoccupied with our plan of retribution. Suddenly, we heard Fatty screaming as he sped his bicycle through the orchard, spilling cherry-size crab apples from the huge pockets of his jungle pants. His speed overtook his ability to steer, and he crashed in a clump of weeds between two plum trees. He raised his grass-stained face and shouted, "He's coming!" We dropped our baseball equipment, ran to the old bench we used as a dugout, grabbed our armaments, and headed for our stations.

15:04:00 hours: We hear the Mr. Softie truck's song, and from the top of a tall pine tree Tommy signals his approach, traveling west on our street.

15:06:15 hours: The target slows at the corner and proceeds by turning north on the side street, it travels thirty feet and stops.

15:06:30 hours: Merrill and Eric, walking toward each other from both corners, pick up two heavy "Caution: Children Playing" barricades and place them behind the target and then disappear in the bushes.

15:08:00 hours: The ice-cream salesman, wondering where all the kids are and curious what the two were doing behind his truck, exits his vehicle and walks to the rear, cursing.

15:09:10 hours: While the salesman is trying to move the heavy barricades, Pete and Donald jump out of the bushes fifty yards in front of the target, carrying a bag of apples and "Big Bertha," a two-man, four-foot-tall slingshot, with stand. They set up in the middle of the side street, facing the front of the target.

15:11:00 hours: The salesman, sensing something is awry, foregoes moving the barricades and heads back to the front of the truck, cursing louder. As he steps up in the truck, he looks over his left shoulder just in time to see Pete lean back, stretching the inner tube back with both hands, his feet pressed to both sides of the slingshot's fork. Donald slips a big green apple in the slings pocket.

15:11:45 hours: "*Flllapp!*" The first salvo is fired. The projectile sizzles through the hot summer air, striking the loud speaker dead center. The Mr. Softie tune still comes out, but now sounds like someone is humming the tune while pinching their nostrils closed.

15:11:50 hours: Fatty blows his whistle and a barrage of crab apples is fired from handheld slingshots by the rest who had been hiding in the surrounding trees and bushes. The quiet summer afternoon is now reverberating with the sound of dozens of the fruit missiles slamming into the sides and roof of the target.

15:12:00 hours: The salesman, stunned by the attack, jumps into the driver's seat just as another salvo from Big Bertha slams into the dividing bar of his windshield, spraying apple juice across the front of his truck. In a panic, the driver punches the accelerator, pops the clutch, and screeches his tires as he heads directly for Pete and Donald. They roll to the sides of the street. As he passes them, they roll back, set up and fire a parting shot, hitting the target square in the center of the rear panel doors.

15:12:30 hours: The girls appear from the shadows of the home's porticoes, cheering, waving scarves and handkerchiefs at their triumphant liberators. A small crowd of soldiers and celebrators circled the pair still manning the big gun. The general and his assistant rise up to face the exhilarated crowd.

Jill, carrying Melissa in her arms, slipped through the gathering and stood next to Pete. Melissa leaned over and kissed Pete on the cheek.

"Thanks, Pete," she said shyly.

Jill slid around his back and kissed him on his other cheek. "You're quite a man," she said coyly.

Pete's face flushed and he hung his head. "Aww, it was nothing."

The next day during the ball game we were all surprised to hear the singsong melody of the Mr. Softie truck. We didn't believe he would have the nerve to return. As a group, biggest up front, we apprehensively approached the side of the new and shiny van. The window quickly slid open. There, on the other side, was the jolliest old guy you'd ever seen. He had the aura of a great big banana split.

"Hello, kids!" he cheered and he held out his arms.

Still stunned, we stood there, speechless. He disappeared for a second and came out of the passenger's door of the van with a big smile and asked, "Now, who is Melissa?" Instinctively, we created a protective wall around her. Curiosity overcame her and she poked her head out between two of the boys.

"I'm Melissa," she said disarmingly.

"Well, I have one of these for you and one for your mother," he announced while holding out an ice-cream sandwich in both hands. "They're from the owner of the company," he said proudly. We all traded stares in disbelief.

"Now, what can I get for the rest of you children?" And all was right with the world again.

So, if you are in sales and you feel the need to intimidate your customers just to make you feel superior, remember this: every job has two bosses; the one who can fire you, and the other one who can tell him to fire you . . . the customer.

A Night Made for Football

The early fall's evening air was cool and crisp. A faint wood smoke haze softened the bright rows of field lights against the coal black September sky. A sea of sparkling emeralds seemed to have been spread over the entirety of the finely manicured and neatly chalked playing field. The aroma of buttered popcorn, grilled hot dogs, warm giant pretzels, and steaming hot cocoa drifted from the concession stand through the mesmerized lines of patrons. Grade-school kids wrestled or just plain rolled in the thick grass of the end zones while others darted through the ranks of Dads who balanced stacks of the delightful treats, making their way back to their impatiently waiting clan. Friends and relatives of the players packed the stands as the cheerleaders and marching band led them in the school's favorite fight song, "Go, Eagles, Go!" It was if there was a competition going on trying to out-dazzle each of the five senses. If you're a lover of football, well, this is the stuff that lines our souls.

The first game of the regular season was still a week away, but tonight's game was always the most attended as it was the preseason scrimmage between the Varsity and the Junior Varsity teams of my mid-western suburban high school.

Because of my average size and strength and being a sophomore, I would have been destined to warm the bench if not for an assistant coach spying me one day on the sidelines at practice, messing around, place-kicking the football. I wanted to be an inside linebacker, but after watching me kick six in a row into the end zone from the forty, he convinced me to take the first string kicking position for the JV team. I enjoyed the prestige of being first string something, and being that the two-a-day summer practices were brutal for defensive backs and all I had to do was kick the ball, made things even more enjoyable.

The referee of this year's preseason game flipped a shiny silver dollar into the night air. Fate had her way and the Varsity won the toss, which meant that I would be the first player of the 1968 season to touch the ball. Before I trotted out onto the field, I looked over my shoulder and spotted my parents in the stands, their faces beaming with pride. I was confident, practiced, and ready. I had no doubt of success. The whistle blew. I waved back to the field judge and approached the ball. There was a drum roll from the marching band and a crash of cymbals as I firmly planted my foot into the focal point of the event, spinning it in a reverse end-over-end fashion. The ball rose into the night, a real beauty. Undisturbed, its trajectory would have landed it past the end zone. Any other receiver would have let it go for a touchback, but not Ben.

Ben Buckler was a magnificent human specimen. At six foot five and two hundred and forty-five pounds, his chiseled muscular body and unbelievable coordination made him the top star of our football, basketball, and track teams. A real competitor with a heart of gold, he was loved by all. Unfortunately, he was somewhat academically challenged and at the age of twenty-one was still trying to graduate.

They came back at us with the standard "V" formation, which means if each of their players did their job, there would be nothing standing between Ben and a glorious touchdown, except me. The thrill of my spectacular kick vanished as I witnessed the horror that filled my view. My teammates, almost at the same instant, were mercilessly leveled by their opponents. Barely trotting now, I looked to the opposite end of the field. There he was, coming straight at me. The ball firmly tucked under his left arm, leaning forward at an angle of about forty-five degrees, he passed the twenty-yard line doing close to thirty miles per hour. Clods of turf filled the air behind his thoroughbred gallop. His eyes were dark and glassy and fixed solely on mine. Twenty yards away he deftly raised the clinched fist of his right arm, his elbow slightly bent; it was the perfect battering ram. I then realized I was an unwitting participant in a modern-day jousting tournament. Totally unprepared for the inevitable carnage, I became engulfed with impending doom.

I only had a moment to think. I then heard the voice of my driver's education teacher in my head. "Do you know why drunks survive more often in horrific automobile crashes than sober people? They're limp, they roll with the punches." Heeding his advice, a microsecond before impact, I went limp, as if every bone in my body disappeared.

"Keerack!" The sound echoed off the astonished observers. It was if a speeding freight train had smacked into a large stack of empty cardboard boxes. The boxes were obliterated and the train didn't slow a bit. I never heard a thing. I only saw the lights above, the field, the grass, the lights again, and on and on it went until finally, only darkness. I was out. I started to come to and tried to open my eyes. My left eye was completely blind accompanied by the strangest sideways tunnel vision in my right, and I seemed to be deaf in my left ear. I could just make out Ben striding back this way from the end zone, the ball raised high over his head in a salute to a strangely quiet crowd. Confused, he saw the group of players, coaches, and others forming at midfield. Then, he saw me, dropped the ball, and starting running to me, faster than before.

Then the pain came . . . from everywhere, especially my head. There was an incredible crushing pain to my nose. Then I blacked out again. I came to and evidently hadn't moved as my angle of view was unchanged. Except this time all I could see were shoes. I saw my coach's shoes and some of the other player's shoes, my mom and dad's shoes, and the school nurses shoes. From my right ear I could hear some of my teammates saying, "How could his legs be that way and his body the other?" and "Look, even his socks are gone!" I heard Ben crying, "Please, God, oh please don't let him die."

Then my coach said, "Alright men, everyone hold his arms and legs still." And then in a voice as gentle as I've ever heard, Coach said to me, "Son, be brave, we're going to try and spin your helmet around now." It became a great relief to me that I was not deaf in one ear and blind in one eye. It was simply Ben hit me so hard that it twisted my helmet around and I had been peering out an ear hole.

The Varsity won that game as they had since the school's very first scrimmage between the two. I didn't play the rest of that game. I think that was agreed upon during a little discussion between Coach, Ben, and my mom. I warmed the bench the rest of the game along with other JV casualties that soon piled up alongside of me. But we still enjoyed being there, in the enchanted palace of the grid iron.

And oh, to be able to go back and experience it all again; the sights, the sounds, the magic of touching a live football, and the smell of the turf. Yes, even when it's shoved up your nose. But I did get to keep something from that night. I learned a valuable lesson of life that I keep with me every day and should be remembered by the competitive sales person who is suiting up for the big game.

When you are confronted with what may be considered overwhelming opposition, be prepared for the battle, don't go limp. Hit them with everything you have. Things might not turn out as bad as you think. At least you let them know you were there.

An Unusual Wrestling Ring

The five of them huddled together on the broad sidewalk. Even though it was a warm, summer, St. Louis afternoon, two of them wore hooded sweatshirts while the others donned long black leather coats. After a brief conference, two of them, in coats, broke away and walked across the street, while the other three entered the large jewelry store. Coach Renn slid the ring tray he had been organizing, back into the display case counter he stood behind and locked its sliding back panel. He rested his large, thick hands on the glass top and watched the three spread out as they came in.

Coach Renn wasn't a tall man, but he was big. His sports jacket, while probably being a sixty regular, stretched tightly around his broad shoulders and huge biceps. He was, after all, the wrestling coach of my high school. He had taken a summer job as a sales clerk at one the cities renowned jewelry stores in an old section of the downtown area. I was a junior and had taken a part-time job with my friend Kirk, working for a large greeting card company. By chance, we had been given the two-day assignment of resetting the card and gift merchandisers in the jewelry store where Coach was working.

It was strange to be working side-by-side as an equal with a teacher, and we teased him about being a hoity-toity jewelry salesman, knowing we would pay dearly for our remarks at the coming year's gym classes. He jokingly said that the he could only take the excitement of this job three months out of the year and couldn't wait to get back to coaching wrestling matches, so he could relax. We all laughed. He had an easygoing personality, when he wanted. He could also be tough as nails.

It was a large establishment, for a jewelry store, probably forty feet deep and eighty feet wide. The front and side of the store were window walls, lined with glass shelves full of fine crystal, china, and silverware. The back wall was fronted with a long, glass, jewelry counter and the remaining wall was nearly hidden by our card and gift merchandisers.

It was our second day there and would have likely wrapped things up by midafternoon if there weren't any hiccups. I saw the three enter the store, too, and noticed Coach keeping a keen eye on them as he walked over to me.

"Hey," he said quietly as he paused and picked out a card, pretending to read it. "See those guys?" I nodded yes. "They were here last week . . . just looked around and left." He picked out another card. "Something's up." He slid the cards back and returned to the jewelry counter.

The store had three other salesmen in it and all were working with other customers. People who work in jewelry stores have a sixth sense about who comes in and out of their store, even if they're busy with customers. As I filed more cards in their proper slots, I glanced at the other three clerks and could tell they too were aware of the suspicious characters. Kirk came back from the rear stock room and I helped him set the heavy box he was carrying on the floor behind one of the merchandisers.

"Don't look up," I whispered. "Coach says something's about to go down."

Kirk popped his head up above the merchandiser like a submarine's periscope.

"No, man!" I hissed and pulled him back down by his collar. "Just keep your eyes open and listen to Coach." I went back to my spot while Kirk popped his head up every five seconds to see what was happening. He was about as stealthy as a jack-in-the-box.

The three meandered around the store aimlessly, inspecting random merchandise. This went on for several minutes when the two with hoodies came from opposite ends of the store and met at the counter in front of Coach.

He gave them a wry smile and said, "What can I do for you gentlemen today?"

"We like to see da rings," grunted one, pointing down to a ring tray in the display case.

"Sure," said Coach, unlocking the sliding panel, removing the tray and locking it back.

At that moment, the bell above the front door chimed and the two who were across the street entered the store and headed for the far end of the counter.

Coach nodded and smiled at them and said, "Be with you in a minute." He set the tray on the counter between him and the two hoodies. "Which one would you like to see?" he said dryly, motioning to the tray where fifty men's diamond rings were neatly pushed down between rows of velvet.

"Um, dat one," said one of the hoodies.

It is traditional for a jeweler to allow a potential customer to try on an expensive ring, and Coach slowly handed him the one he requested. He could see, out of the corner of his eye, the two newcomers were taking gold necklaces off a counter display and inspecting them. He said in a loud but friendly voice, "I'll be with you folks in just a minute!" The other clerks heard this and it perked up their attention.

Just then, the other one in a coat, who had wandered to my end of the store, knocked over a silver tray, that was displayed on one of the glass shelves, which made a loud clanging noise. Two of the clerks walked toward him and told him to step back. He bolted for the front door and dashed out. Coach had taken his eyes off the two in front of him for a second and when he looked back, the ring was gone.

He boomed, "Where's the ring!"

They looked back at him with big eyes and said, "Man, we ain't got yo ring!"

"Johnny, lock the door!" Coach shouted. "Frank, pull the alarm! Dale, close that door!" motioning to the stock room door. "Now, where's my ring!" he shouted again as he deftly slid the tray into a cubby hole behind him, never taking his eyes off them.

"I told you, man. We ain't got yo ring!" and the two held out their empty hands as proof.

Instantly, Coach latched onto a wrist of each with his massive hands. They tried to pull away but he squeezed down on them, and both gave out a cry of pain as they experienced the bulldog grip of a Kansas State wrestling champ.

The other two, by the necklaces, became nervous and walked quickly around the store, erratically. I saw one of them slip a couple of gold necklaces out of his coat pocket and inconspicuously toss them on a shelf and kept walking.

"You can't hold us," said one of the hoodies, defiantly.

"I can until the police get here," and with that they drew back their free hands in fists. Coach grunted, gritted his teeth while clamping down on their wrists with such intensity they fell to their knees, screaming in agony.

In that part of town there were always squad cars in the area, and in a few moments Johnny was unlocking the door to let in two officers. Coach's vice-like grip had the two hoodies paralyzed for over five minutes and, by the determined look on his face, could have lasted for hours. The two that had attempted to steal necklaces had been cordoned off by the other two clerks as their customers gathered quietly by the front door.

When the policemen entered, one immediately went to the aid of Coach by handcuffing the two, and the other went to confront the two in coats. They found the $3,000 ring, which had been slipped into the pants pocket of one of the hoodies. The two in coats denied any wrongdoing until I walked over and told the officer that I saw one of them toss some jewelry out of his possession when the commotion started and pointed to where it landed.

All four were arrested and thanks to Coach's and my testimony, were eventually convicted of attempted robbery.

At the end of the day, when everything returned to normal, Coach came over to talk to Kirk and me.

"You guys did great! You kept your cool and stepped up and did the right things. I'm proud of you!" and he grabbed us in a headlock. He meant it playfully, but it did hurt a little. "I'll bet you never guessed being a salesman could be so exciting!" He was right about that!

Too Good to Be True

The summer had been a busy one. I had worked full-time as an apprentice machinist at a local shop that made construction tools and was paid $6 per hour. In 1970 that was a pretty good wage, and I had saved enough money to buy my first car a week before my senior year started in high school. I had my eye on a used (very used) TR-6 Triumph convertible. A real snazzy sports car that was sure to turn the ladies' heads. Speaking of heads, mine had gained a little altitude as I had grown five inches that summer. "It was too good to be true," I thought. I was going to be a senior, had money for a sports car, and had finally become tall.

As it turned out, I was right. My dad pulled up in the driveway one evening, five days before school started, in a bombshell of a car. It was a 1958 Chevy Biscayne. He said he had taken the money I saved in our joint savings account and bought it for me. He said it was a sturdy car with low mileage and one owner, and it would serve me well for years to come. Indeed, he was right, as it did. But at that moment it was a crushing blow, and I sat on the curb, staring at it, and just cried. I don't think I even touched it for days.

The first day of school came, and I was faced with walking to school or taking "the boat." I decided the latter, as a senior without wheels was considered a nerd. It did turn the heads of the pretty girls, though . . . away! At least I still had two happy thoughts working for me, I mused, as I pulled in the last available spot of the slant parking in front of the school. I was a senior and would relish in the respect deserved from the underclassmen, and I was the second tallest kid in the school. Reconfirming this, I arched my back, stood up straight as a board, and enjoyed the clear view as I towered over the other kids walking to the "old gym."

The old gym was in the main building just beyond the pillared entrance of the school. Once inside the school's front doors and about thirty feet beyond, were the four old wooden French doors to the gym. Just past the French doors was a short but very wide set of stairs that led directly down onto the basketball court. As I entered the school, I could see over everyone's head and spotted a couple of cute girls I hadn't seen all summer, standing on the gym floor near the bottom of the stairs.

Not wanting to miss them I raced through the French doors. I never had to worry about hitting my head on the heavy door closers that hung from the door jambs before, and I didn't this time either. "Bonk!" I hit my forehead squarely on one of them, knocking me flat on my back. My forward momentum was so strong that I slid a couple feet to the stairs and all the way down to the bottom, taking a couple of freshman with me. Sprawled out on my back on the gym floor, intertwined with the freshman, I looked up in a daze at the two pretty girls.

"That's Dale. Always the class clown," they chuckled and walked away.

As inconspicuously as possible, I picked myself up off the floor and looked through the gym. It was full of kids, standing in lines at alphabetically arranged registration tables, half of them looking at me. I spotted the "Senior A-D" table at the far end of the gym and headed in that direction. I tried to act as cool as possible, but most of the kids who saw my entrance were still laughing.

"Stop right there, son!" an older voice commanded behind me. I instantly recognized the voice. It was Coach Pitt. I turned and faced him and another man, Coach Lang, who was standing next to him. Both eyed me over.

"What's your name, son?" queried Coach Pitt.

"It's me, Coach. Dale Dahlin. I was on your football team a couple of years ago. Remember?" I said, my feelings half hurt.

"Oh yeah," said Coach Lang. "Remember, Coach? This was the kid with the helmet problem at the scrimmage game."

"Oh, that's right," said Coach Pitt, and both tried to stifle a laugh.

"Well, you've really grown. Haven't you, son?" Coach Pitt remarked. "What are you, six-three?"

"Six-four," I responded proudly, standing as tall as I could.

"Six-four!" they repeated in unison, their eyes gleaming. "Come with us, son. This registration stuff can wait," Coach Pitt directed, and they led me to the side door. "Watch your head," they laughed as they held the door open for me. They walked in front of me as we went through the courtyard, heading for the "new gym." As we walked, they strategized.

"We could move Smith to guard and Jones to center. That would leave a forward spot open, if we used a 2-1-2 offence," said one. "That just might work," replied the other.

They unlocked the door to the gym, and we walked to the top of one of the keys. The lights were off, but huge beams of sunlight were steaming through the windows that lined the top of one wall, providing more than sufficient lighting. They turned and faced me.

"Alright son, jump up and see how high you can reach your hand over the rim," one instructed. "You can take a running start, if you want."

I looked at them and then to the backboard. I walked under the rim, bent down, and jumped as high as I could. "Swish!" My hand barely brushed the bottom of the net.

I looked at the coaches, whose optimistic looks had been replaced with scowls.

"Quit playing around, son. We're serious," said Pitt.

"No, no, Coach," interrupted Lang. "He's cold. He's not warmed up yet."

"Okay, take a couple of laps and do some knee bends," ordered Pitt.

I took my jacket off and laid it on the bleachers, and everything began to come together for me. "I could be a starter for the Varsity Basketball Team," I thought with amazement. "This was too good to be true!"

I ran like the wind around the gym and did a couple of deep knee bends and hustled back to the coaches, still standing in their original spot.

"I'm ready, Coach," I announced. "I think I'll take that running start." Lang was right, I was cold, but now I was loose and warmed up. I too was excited to see how high I could reach over the rim.

I took four giant steps and bounded skyward with all my strength. "*Swish!*" I barely brushed the bottom of the net, no higher than before. I looked back at the coaches whose faces only reflected the defeat of the moment.

"Okay, son," one said after a lengthy pause. "You can go back now," and they walked silently off to their office, leaving me alone in the empty, cheerless gymnasium.

I got back in line at the old gym and tried to bring back some of the optimism I started the day with. "Okay, my car wasn't the hottest thing around and maybe being tall isn't all it's made out to be, either," I went on in my head. "But, I'm still a senior, and I'm going to be 'King of the Hill' around the underclassmen."

I was beginning to feel better about things when I recognized one of the freshmen I accidentally knocked down earlier, standing right in front of me. He looked up at me with half terror and half determination in his eyes. He quickly lifted up his hands and pushed me in the chest. Stunned at this, I tried to step back to keep my balance, but something prevented my feet from moving backward. I fell over the other freshman who was on his hands and knees behind me. Sprawled, once again, on my back on the gym floor, I looked up in a daze at the two, both shaking each other's hand and smiling.

"And that's what you get for trying to make us look like idiots on our first day of high school, ya big jerk!" said one, looking down at me. And they walked away while some of their classmates cheered triumphantly.

I learned several things that day. Sometimes life sets you up, just to knock you down. No matter how optimistic you feel about something, sometimes it's wise to keep that feeling guarded. And lastly, things usually have a way of working themselves out for the better. For instance, I didn't play for the basketball team. But I did get to sit in the bleachers with the pretty girls during the games and got to snuggle with them to keep them warm while driving them home in my big car. I never got even with those two freshmen. Instead, we became the best of friends after high school and pal'd around for years. So I guess the old saying, "Things that are too good to be true, usually are" isn't always correct, because I know of a few instances where they turned out better.

Getting "The Job"

"Just take a seat over there, honey," said the receptionist, as she peered through the small open window while pointing to the waiting area next to her little booth. I took a few steps in the direction she pointed and took a seat on the old Naugahyde couch in the small waiting area. The only other seat in the room was a matching side chair occupied by a well-dressed, nice-looking young woman who nodded and smiled briefly at me as I sat down. She went back to her magazine as I unbuttoned my suit jacket and noticed my seat felt unusually cool. I looked down to inspect the material I was sitting on and to my horror discovered that I wasn't wearing any pants, just my shoes, socks, and boxers. "Oh no!" I panicked, "It's happened again!"

I glanced around to the adjoining office area and to my surprise found the people there hadn't noticed me. They just continued to work at their desks, talking on telephones or each other. I looked back to the young woman, still engrossed in her magazine, and instantly realized she had a striking resemblance to my first-grade teacher, Miss Brown. I jumped up from the couch, which made the sound of someone sucking in a big breath while pulling a stretch off a roll of masking tape, and suddenly had the terrific urge to pee.

Miss Brown looked up from her *Think and Do* book and said quietly, "The restroom is down the hall, sweetie."

I dashed around the corner of the waiting area's partition and headed for the front door, instead. But it disappeared and had been replaced with a long hallway. I turned to look back where I came from and found the hallway stretching that way, as well. I felt cold and tried to button my jacket, but it was gone, along with my shirt. I heard my name being called and someone pushed me on the shoulder from behind. I turned, but no one was there.

"Dale!" the voice said again, only louder, and I was shoved in the back a second time and the lights in the hallway went out.

"Dale!" I saw my wife standing over me, holding a wad of covers in her arms. "Wake up! You'll be late for your interview!"

I laid there a moment, trying to catch my breath. "It was that dream again," I said finally, struggling to sit up.

"Don't forget," she said, ignoring my comment. "Come home right after your interview so you can take me to work," she instructed, while stuffing the covers in a laundry basket.

We had only been married a few months and had just moved to Florida. She had found a decent job, working in a gift shop at a local amusement park, and I was still trying to find something that could turn into a career. I actually had already found a job, but I really wasn't thrilled about becoming a copier salesman. My background was in residential construction, and I wanted to sell building materials for a large distributor.

Applying for the job from the copier company was somewhat intimidating. The sales manager was a tough, lean-looking guy in his thirties and wore a banker's suit.

"I got four things I tell my salesmen," he snarled, leaning forward over his desk, staring at me. "You gotta be tough, or they'll eat you alive. You don't take 'No' for an answer. If they throw you out . . . well, you just go back in there the next day, never give up! And if you only make a dozen calls a day, you might be foolin' yourself that you're working, but you're not foolin' me!" He leaned back in his chair, picked up the "fill in the circle" answer card from the personality profile test I had just taken, and said, "Now, let's see how you did."

Even though the card just contained the question numbers and the circles to be filled in, he had evidently memorized what the questions and possible answers were for the first three.

"Aw, ya see kid," he said disappointedly, "I don't think you have what it takes." He studied the card to make sure he was accurate. "You said you'd rather listen to a symphony than lead a marching band, and would want to watch an old favorite movie than go dancing, and would like to walk your dog instead of taming a lion." He put the card down.

"Well, yes, I would, but—" I started to explain.

He interrupted, "We'll run the rest of the hundred questions through the machine and see what it says, but I wouldn't hold out much hope." He stood up and thrust out his hand. "Nice to meet ya, kid. Good luck out there!"

I was shaken by the abrupt ending to the interview and didn't have the chance to tell him I had figured out "how" to take the test on the forth question. I answered the first three questions the way I truly felt, not how a triple "A" salesman would. The remaining questions I answered as if I were Dale Carnegie. I didn't go back and change my first three answers because I was using an ink pen.

Deflated, I headed home to tell my wife about my lousy interview. But I had to agree, he was right about the "four things." The next interviewers were going to have their hands full. The following morning I got a call from the copier company Sales Manager.

"Kid! I mean, Dale! You got the best score we've ever had, 97 out of 100," he sounded as excited as a sportscaster announcing the winning home run. "You'll start two weeks from Monday, when our training classes begin." I was happy and relieved to have gotten a job. But it really wasn't what I was looking for and had two weeks to find something I did want.

Baker & Company was where I felt I could make a career. They were a highly recommended, well-established distributor of quality goods. I had finally gotten to the right man at Baker on the phone and had arranged a "face-to-face" with him the following Monday.

I arrived at their home office a full thirty minutes before the interview. I walked in the front door and instinctively turned left to the receptionist's booth. A tremendous feeling of "déjà vu" came over me as I stood at the small open window.

"I'm here to meet with Mr. Castleberry," I timidly announced through the window.

The middle-aged, buxom woman acknowledged me while she answered the phone on her switchboard. As she answered several more calls, she noticed I was constantly glancing down to my pants. She finally took off her headset, stood up, and leaned over to look out the window between us.

"What are you looking at," she said quizzically.

I had been looking down and didn't notice her new position. "Oh!" I said, startled. "I was . . . a . . . just checking to see if I was . . . a . . . wearing any pants. Ya see. I have this dream . . ."

She fell back to her seat and clutched her chest with folded arms. "Oh my, you have that dream, too? I have it all the time, except it's my top!" and we laughed, a little embarrassed. She cleared her throat, put her business face back on, and said, "Just have a seat over there, honey," and pointed to the waiting area next to her booth.

I took a seat on the eerily familiar Naugahyde couch and said out loud, "Thank God," as I spied Miss Brown was not sitting in the matching chair.

"There's not much to your résumé, is there, son?" lamented Jay Castleberry.

"I'm just twenty-four, sir. I know I don't have much history, but I'm ready to make some."

"Well, tell me a little about yourself," he said, leaning back in his chair.

I was disappointed they didn't use a personality profile test, as I knew I could ace that. Jay was a likable man, twice my age and loved to talk. When I found he had a good sense of humor, we ended up trading jokes for an hour.

Finally he said, "Well, we really don't have any sales openings at this time. But I'll check with the big bosses to make sure."

"Can I check back with you tomorrow, to see?" I said, sitting anxiously on the edge of my chair.

"Sure, that would be fine."

The next morning I was sitting in their waiting area when Jay stepped in the front door at 8:00 a.m. He was surprised to see me sitting there and motioned me into his office.

"I meant you could call me to see what our answer was," he said with a smile. "I didn't intend for you to show up."

"Well, sir. I intend to keep showing up until I get the job. I never give up!" I said proudly.

And show up, I did. Every day that week I sat on that couch waiting for him to come to work. Each day he politely told me "No," they didn't have an opening for me. Finally, Friday, I could see his patience was wearing down.

"Look, kid," he said, drumming his fingers on his desk. "If I tell you 'No' again, and you come back, I'm going to have you arrested for harassment!"

"Well, sir," I said with an exaggerated smile, "I guess I'll see you Monday."

"Sheesh!" he groaned, throwing up his hands. He picked up the phone and punched a button. "Marvin!" he shouted. "I got this kid here I was telling you about. I'm going to send him to you. Either hire him or call the Sheriff. I don't care which!"

"Thanks, Mr. Castleberry!" I exploded, shaking his hand profusely with both of mine. "I know where his office is!" and I rushed out of the room.

I stood outside Marvin's door, composed myself for a moment, insuring I was wearing pants. I knocked on the door and entered. Marvin sat poised and erect behind a large desk covered with neatly stacked reports, invoices, and the six-inch-thick Baker catalog, sitting on a stand, facing him.

"Sit!" He motioned to a chair facing his desk. "Look," he started, "we don't have any openings at this time, and if we did, we only hire salesmen with years of experience. You may be a ballsy kid, but you don't know nothin'!"

I slid to the edge of my chair and clasped my knees with my hands. "Well, I have half the battle won, don't I?" Having nothing to lose, I continued by putting my hand on the catalog. "And if you give me one of these for a month, I'll come back and tell you anything you want to know about it!" Our eyes locked in a dead stare for at least a minute.

He eased his posture, slightly. "Okay, kid," he resigned. "I'll call you sometime next week. If you come back before I call, I'll have you arrested. Got it?!"

"Got it!" I shot back.

The next week came and went without a call. By Friday afternoon I had resolved I would become the best copier salesman in the world and prepared to start that career Monday morning.

At a quarter to five the phone rang while we were changing clothes to go out to dinner. It was Marvin. He said just seven words.

"You got the job. Be here, Monday," and hung up.

I looked in the mirror. I was just wearing my boxers. "How ironic," I said.

"Ironic or not, just get dressed!" my wife ordered.

"Yes, boss," I replied, smiling.

Time with Marvin

I had been with a wholesale building material distributor in Florida for just six months. I had been training for an outside sales position. Although young and inexperienced in the building material industry, I had taken every opportunity to learn all I could about our company and its products and felt I was able to tackle the position of a territorial salesman. As luck would have it, one of our veteran salesmen thought the grass was greener on the other side and, presto, a position was available. As soon as I heard about it, I walked into the sales manager's office and announced that I was ready to fill the spot.

Buck, a gruff old cuss, was almost horizontal, leaning back in his chair with his feet up on the desk, puffing on a cigar.

"Ready?" he said, somewhat surprised and amazed. He studied me for a moment, then sat up, and in a rapid-fire style snapped off a half dozen questions on products, procedures, pricing, and policies. I must have answered them correctly because he punched an intercom button on his desk and said, "Marvin, I want you to spend a little time with someone today." Marvin was the Sales Promotion Manager and often filled in a territory until a permanent salesman was found. Marvin entered the room a minute later. He was the same age as Buck, taller, a better dresser, and somewhat more polished, or so I thought.

"Dahlin? You're sending me out with Dahlin?" he asked arrogantly.

Buck, somewhat annoyed by Marvin's inferred critique of his judgment, responded, "He could hardly screw up more than you."

37

They had worked together for years and this kind of banter was customary. Marvin turned on his heal, looked at me sharply, and said, "You're driving. We're leaving in five minutes," and walked out of the room.

"That's just great," I thought. "Going to call on my first customer with Marvin, who's already got it in for me."

There was a brief pause and searching for some way to break the silence, I asked Buck, "Is there any last bit of advice you want to give me before I go?"

"Yeah," he said, leaning back to his relaxed position and relighting his cigar with a big wooden match. "Don't break wind in the customer's office." There was another pause. "Now, close the door."

"Oh, boy," I thought, "he's really going to tell me a few of the secrets of successful selling." So, I jumped up, closed the door, and sat back down. I was all ears.

"No," he said. "Close the door . . . with you on the other side of it."

Somehow, I knew right then that I really didn't need anyone's help. I should have tried to convince him I would do better alone. But, regretfully, I didn't.

Marvin decided our first call would be on Fastco Lumber located in a little town about fifty miles from our office. It was getting close to noon, and he decided we would stop and have lunch at a little greasy spoon he knew of before we made the call. He had the Blue Plate Special, "All the way." Being a tad bit nervous, I just had some iced tea. The Blue Plate was some kind of road-kill with onions and peppers piled on top. "All the way" meant it had an extra ladle of gravy poured over the whole mess.

"A brave man with a cast iron stomach," I thought. "Or just a glutton." Either way, he finished the entire thing.

Fastco Lumber was a tiny old-fashioned lumber yard that had been around for a hundred years. There were three men who worked it. There was the owner, Bernard, his brother Hedrick, and their faithful employee, Mr. Francis. Each was older than the other. All had long past their seventies. They always dressed in white long-sleeved shirts and dark slacks and wore long, skinny black ties. Bernard, the youngest at eighty-five, sometimes felt sporty and wore a short-sleeved shirt. There was a single door in the front and a small door on the side. We entered the front door. I found out later, vendors were supposed to use the side door.

Immediately to our left was the office and sales counter. Behind the counter were two roll-top desks with wooden swivel chairs and an old heavy oak chair in the corner. Bernard occupied the first desk and chair and was speaking on the phone. Hedrick seemed to be frozen, standing beside his roll-top, and Mr. Francis was semi-dozing in the oak chair while trying to complete his want-list.

"We're with Baker & Company," announced Marvin.

"Shhhh!" replied Hedrick, thawing from his frozen state. "Bernard is on the telephone." Bernard cut his eyes to us and then back to his desktop.

It was a hot day and the air was very still. Save for the occasional comments from Bernard's phone conversation, there wasn't a sound. I set my leather handled peddlers catalog on the floor, and it slightly raised the head of an old bulldog I hadn't noticed sleeping at the feet of Mr. Francis.

At first I wasn't sure what it was. That sound, familiar but . . . there it was again, a growling gurgle. This time it was unmistakable. It was Marvin's stomach or regions there about. "No, no. It certainly couldn't be that," I thought. "Not here. Not now. I mean Marvin was a pro. He wouldn't violate the prime directive that was just given to me by our leader."

And suddenly, there it was—a three-and-a-half second beauty. It would have made any 6th-grade boy proud, or brought down the house in a college lecture hall. And I had to contend with it on my first sales call.

Bernard snapped his eyes at Marvin once again. "Quiet, I'm on the telephone."

Hedrick glared at Marvin. Mr. Francis woke up, somewhat startled, and looked at Marvin. Even the dog raised his head, snorted and sneezed, then got up, and walked out of the room. The silence was deafening. What could I do? I resigned to the urge and also stared at Marvin.

Finally, Marvin, feeling that some response was needed to defend him, said quite plainly, "My shoe made that noise."

Without missing a beat, Hedrick said, "You need new shoes."

I don't recall if we were able to sell anything to them. I was just happy to get out of there without having to give them my business card. In the car, I told Marvin I thought I got the hang of things and wouldn't need any more of his help.

A word of advice to you young fledgling salespeople; if you know you can do something yourself, listen to your conscience. Otherwise, you may end up spending time with Marvin.

A Real Attention Getter

I was a greenhorn outside sales rep for a Florida-based building material distributor and had been calling on customers for only a month. I was just starting to feel comfortable going into a customer's business, introduce myself, and begin the never-ending process of becoming a valuable component of their organization.

It takes years of hard work in learning an account's business, personnel, and customer base in order to find the best fit for your products in their general offering. Relationship building is the key to success. Once you earn the trust and friendship of your customer, and if your products allow him to generate profitable sales, then it's a beautiful thing.

We've all seen movie depictions of the flashy-dressing, smooth-talking salesman that could charm their way past the receptionist and clerks, past the other waiting competing vendor sales reps, make it into the decision maker's office, and walk away with all the business. In thirty years of selling, I've seen it foolishly attempted several times, always with disastrous results. Well, almost always.

It was a bright, cool, and dry November Monday morning. The hot muggy days of summer had begrudgingly lost their grip of the west coast of Florida. Autumn was finally here, which only added more energy to my youthful demeanor and optimism. I had just spent my first four weeks of making sales calls by following the conscripts of my sales mentor and our Sales Promotion Manager, Marvin. He had supplied me with a stack of 5 × 7 note cards, each one having the vital information of the particular customers in my territory. It also had the names of fifty manufacturers we represented and a little check-off box next to each. I was to check the ones we had the potential to sell to that particular customer. There were more questions on the back and when completed would develop a profile of that customer. Boring as hell! After four weeks of trying to gather the information for the cards, I felt I was just spinning my wheels and getting nowhere fast. Most of the customers were nice (a few weren't), and trying to find the right person to answer a particular question was difficult. They were all very busy, or at least acted that way when I approached them, and didn't show any interest in my little cards or the questions on them. "Oh," the third person that I had been passed off to would say, "Fred's the guy who can answer that, and he's off until a week from Thursday." I would hear snickering coming from the others I had queried and found out weeks later there was no Fred.

This day was going to be different. I was going to unveil myself to my largest potential customer, command attention, make a lasting impression of who I was, and get some answers for that damn card!

So, with my best dress slacks, starched sky blue Oxford shirt, and flashy yellow London Fog jacket (it was the late 1970s after all), I strode through the parking lot and headed for their main office. Armed with a smattering of knowledge I carried in my thirty-five-pound peddlers catalog in one hand and a big jar of Hershey's kisses in the other, I sauntered up to the receptionist desk, plopped the chocolates down right in the middle of her paperwork, and blurted, "Good morning, gorgeous!"

This took Gladys a little by surprise, and she jerked back a couple of inches. She raised her head while pushing her upper false teeth back into position. Looking over the horned-rimmed glasses that had slid to the end of her nose, she said, in a thick Brooklyn accent, "Who are ya, and what do ya want?" Not giving a moment to distraction, I said, "I'm here to see the boys," and turned on my heel and toe and strut away.

The boys, as I called them, were six of the best contractor salesmen my customer employed, and they all had their desks in one small office called the "Bull Pen". It was a 12' × 15' windowless room lined with three desks on each side, facing the walls, and there was a short filing cabinet by the entrance. Not wanting to lose any momentum I skirted past the sales counter, where a couple of my competitors were killing time talking to each other while waiting to see the corporate Purchasing Agent. "That's the old way of selling," I convinced myself. I knew if I charmed the contractor sales reps to push my products to their customers, the PA would have no choice but to buy them from me. My rapid advance on the room ended with an abrupt halt at the entrance. All of the contractor salesmen were there, busy as heck, talking to their customers on the phone or to each other. I stood there for a moment to surmise the situation and then went in to action.

"May I have your attention," I nearly shouted, wearing a big smile.

Surprised, the few that weren't already partially facing me, turned their swivel chairs to view the source of the interruption. The silence was golden. This was the immediate and attentive audience I was hoping for. I spoke aloud again while raising my large catalog by its handles, turned just so, in order that all would see my company's name emblazoned on its cover, and aimed to land it on an open corner of the short filing cabinet next to me.

"My name is Dale Dahlin and I'm your new representative from Baker & Company." With that, I plopped the huge book down on the cabinet. Unfortunately, the corner of my catalog caught the edge of a large flat toolbox that contained thousands of tiny pieces of metal pins used in keying door knobs. The pins came in dozens of different sizes, all in little different compartments covered by the latched lid of the box. The box was sitting not quite all the way on top of a stack of brochures, which made for a perfect fulcrum. The weight of the descending catalog flipped the still closed box high in the air, right toward the center of the room. Time snapped in to slow motion. My pathetic attempt to grab it with my free hand in mid-air only made matters worse by catching the box's latch with my little finger, flipping the latch open.

"Oh!" groaned several of the group, familiar with this type of accident.

"Bushzow!" the box hit the terrazzo floor with a front corner and completely popped open. All of the thousands of pins, micro-springs, and mini-clips shot in all directions across the floor under my audience and their desks. As the last of the particulates found their resting place over the entirety of the floor, six sets of eyes lifted from the chaos and gazed at my sheepish grin. Finally, one of them said matter-of-factly, "Dale . . . from Baker . . . got it."

I spent the rest of that morning and much of the afternoon on my hands and knees, scooping up the pins and things that had just gone everywhere and re-sorting them back into the proper compartments of that dreadful box. The salesmen, undaunted by the event, went back to their phone calls and conversations. Business quickly got back to usual with their builder customers coming in to drop off plans and ask questions and other employees coming in to discuss all facets of their daily business. With each intruder that would come in and have to step around me, the question was asked, "What happened here?" And the answer would always be, "The new kid . . . Dale . . . from Baker, dropped the keying kit." "Ooh," they would all moan as I timidly raised my hand up to shake theirs and ask their name.

As I carried on with my cleaning task, I couldn't help from listening to their dialogue. I felt like a bat-boy in the dugout of a pro baseball team. I learned more in those four or five hours than I had in the entire four weeks prior. When I got back to my car, I took out Marvin's 5 × 7 card and filled out every last section, and then some.

At the weekly review of my travels, Marvin was astounded at the detail and accuracy of this particular customer's sales potential evaluation.

"How did you get such valuable information from this customer?" he asked as he held up the card in amazement.

I leaned back in the chair and cocked my head to the side and said, "Charm, Marvin . . . just pure and simple charm."

What'll It Be, Kid?

"Who do you think you are, kid? Coming in here and telling me what I have to pay and not pay!" demanded Jim as he pressed his large hands flat on the counter between us. "I bought this junk from your company and it didn't sell!" he continued. "I want you to take it back, and I'm not going to pay any restocking charges!"

This was not at all the way I intended my first call on Rockman's Paint and Supply to go. One of the product lines my company handled was a popular brand of house paints and stains. There were many premixed colors offered in the different categories and not all sold as well as the others. The previous salesman in my territory had probably mentioned this during the initial sale. Even then, there are those customers who bite off more than they can chew and think they can bully their way to get the distributor to take back slow-moving and sometimes shop-worn products for full credit. I had many paint store accounts in my territory, and the vast majority of them did very well with this line. But Rockman's Paint was a small, remotely located enterprise in a sparsely populated county, and well, let's just say, his sales of our goods were lackluster at best.

Jim was a tall, thickly built, intimidating man with hairy, almost furry, forearms and knuckles. His sloping forehead and jaunting chin suggested that his lineage was more than a few generations closer to our Stone Age predecessors than the average man. Only his scarlet-tinted glasses pierced by his beady eyes gave him any resemblance to a modern man.

I had to think quickly and call on my limited sales experience to defuse this awkward confrontation. Setting down the piece of paper from which

I had just recited our Return Goods Policy, I soothingly spoke, "Mr. Rockman, Jim, may I? Again, our return policy is of a standard nature in our industry. We have costs of storing, shipping, and promoting our products. Competition is keen in this business and profits are meager. That's why we are forced to charge a minimal 15 percent restocking fee for items that are returned to us, unless of course, we shipped something to you that you didn't order."

My little speech didn't garner nearly the response I had experienced previously when I presented it to other customers. I noticed beads of sweat forming on his forehead, filtering through his hedge-like uni-brow and running down his bulbous nose. I thought I saw steam starting to rise from the back of his sun-burnt, crinkly neck. His lips were drawn so tight that his mouth almost became invisible. His massive hands, still pressed down on the counter, began to clench into fists; the thick, cracked fingernails scratching the countertop as they went.

Sensing this sales call was about to come to an end, I slipped my hand down the side of the stool I was sitting on and felt for the leather handles of my suitcase-like catalog. My eyes wide and locked onto his, I ever so gently began to lift my tense body from the stool. And then it came. The hurricane force of hot, wet wind that came from his mouth, blew me the rest of the way off the back of the stool.

"No, you may not call me Jim!" he shouted. "You can take your *stinking* Returned Goods Policy and get the *heck* out of my store!"

Actually, he used other words than "stinking" and "heck." While I was continuing my backward advance to the front door, propelled by his eruption, he wadded up the trouble-making policy page and my order form that was under it and threw them at me with both hands over his head. It reminded me of what a gorilla would do with a rock or coconut against a threatening intruder. Thank goodness it was an out-swinging door, although I would have gone through it anyway. I landed in the parking lot with my catalog still in hand and Jim's missile on the ground in front of me. I didn't hesitate to pick it up. I simply dove in my car and screeched out of the parking lot, never to return.

It took months, no—years, for the emotional wounds to heal that were inflicted that day. How could I have handled it better? Why didn't our previous salesman do a better job in explaining our policies when he took the order? Or maybe, why was it that Jim was just simply a mean bully? I thought the scars that were left would never go away until one of life's devilish sweetness's was presented on my plate, one fine day.

A half a dozen years had passed, and I had seasoned a bit as a salesman and had learned to better handle adversity with unreasonable people. I had even become somewhat adept at manipulating confrontational people and pretty much having my way with them, just for sport.

This particular July afternoon was hotter than most and I was parched. I had just completed my last call of the day and had a thirty-minute drive in front of me. The big "99 Cent Slushy" sign in the window of the "Kwiky-Mart" lured me in, and in a trance I plodded to the Slushy dispensing machine. "Ahhh!" That first sip of icy-liquid sweetness was exhilarating, and I loved showing my blue tongue to my kids when I got home.

I set the sixty-four-ounce cup on the sales counter and dug in my pants pocket for some change. I happened to glance up to look at the clerk and my eyes met the scarlet-tinted, beady-eyed stare of "him." Oh yes, we recognized each other immediately. With every intent to intimidate me, Jim leaned over and put his big hairy hands flat on the counter between us. I froze for a second. Then he said in a low growl, "What'll it be, kid?"

Surprisingly, a calming wave of cool placidity came over me. "Oh my," I thought. "Jim's had a bit of hard luck and has now found himself serving me, as a clerk, in a convenience store." I remembered all of the horrible, scary feelings I experienced with our first meeting. Retributions were in order, I determined. Quickly, gathering the available assets of my surroundings to mount an onslaught of my adversary, I noticed a couple of other customers had lined up behind me at the register. A nice audience, I thought. Directly behind Jim, turned sideways, was a short, stout fellow in a suit with a little "Kwiky-Mart" pin on his lapel. He was counting cigarette packs and checking things off on a clipboard in his hands. "Ahh, yes," I thought, "the authoritative figure, to keep things peaceful."

I eased my stance a bit and took a long hit off the Slushy. Not as a question, but more as an analysis in semantics; I looked about a foot over his head and drawled out the statement, "What'll it be, kid." The pen in "the suits" hand instantly quit scratching on the clipboard and turned his head just slightly in my direction. Again, I repeated the dangling question, this time even slower and a little louder, as if to really hear the words more distinctly. "*Whaddle it beeee, kid?*"

Jim's massive hands started their fist-clenching routine. The customers behind me started showing interest in the play unfolding before them. "The suit" turned a bit more and set down the clipboard. I lowered my gaze and took notice of Jim's cute little short-sleeved smock with all the tiny little "Kwiky-Mart" logos all over it. With his furry arms sticking out, it looked like someone had dressed up a chimp for one of their TV commercials. Fearless now, I reached out and tilted the corner of his name tag so that I could read it. "Jim," I said plainly. "Your name is Jim."

Sweat started forming on his brow.

"You know, Jim," I continued. "I've been in hundreds and hundreds of 'Kwiky-Mart' stores, and I don't think I've ever heard that 'Official' greeting before." I paused a moment. "I think it lacks a little professionalism, don't you . . . Jim?"

Jim's lips pursed tightly, and I thought I could see steam staring to rise off the back of his neck. He leaned a little more forward and now had more weight on his hands than his feet. The sound came from deep within his primal chest. "Are you gonna buy that thing or not?" he grunted. The other patrons shifted around to get a better view of the spectacle. Undaunted, I pressed on.

"Whatever happened to, 'Welcome to Kwiky-Mart. How may I help you?'" I said in a sing-song voice. "I think that one works nicely. What do you think . . . Jim?"

"The suit", seeing his aggressive stance and fearing Jim might pounce upon me, quickly sidled up to him and inconspicuously tried to scoot him over. But Jim had turned to stone.

"The suit" apologized profusely, "I'm sorry, sir. Jim's been with us only a short time and I don't know what's gotten into him. Tell you what, how about your drinks on him?" And he turned to face him. "Right . . . Jim?"

I leaned over and stared him directly in the face. "Golly," I said cheerfully. "That's great! Thanks, . . . Jim!"

I waltzed out of the store and floated into the driver's seat of my car. As I watched the last of the other customers leave, I saw "the suit" face Jim and raise his flailing arms above his head in disgust of his performance. I watched the ranting continue for a couple more moments and then drove home, feeling the scars from my initial encounter with him dissolve.

I knew I would never have a Slushy as sweet as the one I had that day, but that didn't stop me from trying. I went back to that store several more times but my friend was never around. When I enquired as to his employment, I was told, "He just moved on."

"Uh-oh," I thought. "I sure hope he doesn't get back into the paint business!"

The Right Call

"Hey batter, batter . . . hey batter, batter . . . Swing!" I yelled from the dugout, my fingers clinging to the chain-link fence surrounding it.

Amy's hesitated swing missed the ball by a foot as it skimmed across home plate. She shot a confused look at me as I felt someone jab their elbow in my side.

"Knock it off, Dad!" my ten-year-old daughter commanded, standing next to me. "She's on our team!"

I knew that. I also knew I was hot and tired, and we were in extra innings of the first game of the elimination tournament. When I volunteered to the Assistant Coaching spot on my daughter's fast-pitch soft ball team, I didn't expect its spring season to stretch out into summer. But, our girls just kept on winning.

"I'm just kidding, honey," I grunted, holding my side.

"You'd better be!" she scolded as she turned away to join her teammates at the other end of the dugout. The other girl's fiery stares faded away from me and back to the game as they started another of their endless cheers.

The ten-week season of the ten to twelve-year-olds Northside Fast-Pitch Softball League had long passed, and we were in the third week of post season play. I missed having my usual weekends, going fishing or working on pet projects around the house, interrupted by an occasional nap. And I missed my cold beer that I found out was *not allowed* in the ballpark complex and was instructed *not* to bring back.

"*Boink*," rung Amy's aluminum bat as it crunched the ball, soaring it deep into left field.

"Go foul, go foul," I mouthed, knowing it would be the second strike of the third out for our team, finally ending the season.

My daughter glared at me and shouted "Dad!" in a very condescending voice.

"I'm saying, 'Go fair, go fair,'" I defended as the ball just missed the foul post and went over the fence for a home run. "And look, it did!" as I forced an unconvincing smile on my face.

The team whooped with joy as Amy trotted down the first base line. Coach Johnson and the rest of the team surrounded home plate as the girl who was already on base jumped on home plate to tie the game and then turned to greet Amy, whose run won it. They all jumped up and down high-fiving and hugging each other as I collected the bats and rest of the equipment, stuffing it unceremoniously in large canvas bags. With the bags slung over my shoulders, I headed for the next field and the next game when I was met by Amy's beaming face, sporting an ear-to-ear smile. I looked down at the glowing ten-year-old and returned a genuine smile.

"That was one terrific hit!" I said proudly. "Congratulations honey."

"Thanks, coach," she said appreciatively. "I just did like you've been showing me at practice," and she gave me a big hug.

I blinked back a tear and said, "Now go and celebrate with your teammates," as she turned and ran back to them. "Tell them to be at Field 5 by three-thirty," as the next game began at four, "and go easy on the soda pop!"

I sat the bags in the visitor's dugout and took a seat on its long wooden bench in the shade. Pulling my cap over my eyes and leaning back against the cool concrete wall, I settled in for a bit of a rest. Visions of frosty, crystal mugs pirouetting in a scene of a wintry ballet filled my mind. They would take turns waltzing under an icy water-fall of crisp, cold beer filling themselves to the brim. Then, one by one, they would slide across a long, narrow frozen pond to a Giant who would pick them up and happily guzzle down their contents and slide them back for more. This went on for some time when a voice came from the clouds above.

"Coach?" it said.

The mugs slid to a halt and looked up. A small break in the clouds began to form, spilling a bright light across the scene.

"Coach?" is said again, only louder.

The mugs, frightened by this, began to scurry for cover behind the frosty celery trees and salt-covered mounds of pretzels, spilling their contents. The light became brighter and brighter.

"Coach Dahlin!" the voice boomed like thunder. The giant angrily looked up to the blinding light.

"What do you want!?" I growled. "Oh . . . it's you, Amy," I reconciled.

"Coach Johnson wants to see you at home plate with the umpire," she stated, still holding up the bill of my cap.

"Oh . . . okay," I replied, trying to compose myself. "You startled me a little," I said as I got up and patted her on the head.

I ran in to Coach Johnson half way to home plate as he was headed back to our dugout.

"Sorry, I missed the meeting," I said. "What's up?"

"Oh, it's just the second umpire isn't going to show," he said, "And we . . ."

"Need to cancel the game!" I interrupted eagerly.

"No," he laughed, knowing my anxiousness to call it a day.

"We have to furnish a replacement for him," he continued. "And I volunteered you."

"Me!? I don't even know all of the rules!"

"You just have to stand behind second base and make any tag calls. He'll handle home plate and the rest. Just call 'em like you see 'em," and he walked off to the dugout. He turned and laughed, "Oh yeah, you can't root for our team . . . or theirs."

The winner of this game would be the league champion and would have a seat in the state championship. That would mean more weekends, driving a van full of jabbering girls one hundred miles to the game and one hundred miles back. I shuttered at the thought of it.

The home plate ump gave me a black cap and black T-shirt to wear so that I wouldn't show partiality to our team. I didn't slip into the shirt. Because it was a 3X, I climbed into it and pulled it down past my knees. I would have felt like a rapper, but there wasn't any rap back then. Ahh . . . those were the days!

I knew I was in for a grueling afternoon, standing in the hot sun in what resembled a black Tee-Pee. The game began in front of a capacity crowd and some of the parents jokingly yelled, "Kill the umpire!" recognizing me behind second base.

Luckily, the game became a pitcher's duel and went rather quickly, and I hadn't been forced to make any calls. The final inning came and the pitchers on both teams began to wilt. Neither team had any relief pitchers left and the bats started to sing. Our team commenced to sting the ball in the top of the inning and when they were done, had created three runs. Thoughts of long drives to the championship games filled my head and I became sullen and even angry. You know, just like a real umpire.

The other team responded quickly and in a few minutes they had two runs, a runner on second and just one out. My selfish thoughts drifted away as I became engrossed in what was surely headed to be thriller.

The coach of the other team had put himself in a real quandary. League rules required the coaches to play all of their players in each game and he had one player who had not seen any action. He paced the dugout as the home plate ump yelled "Batter up!" Knowing that if his next regular batter made an out, the last chance to save the season would rest on his littlest girl, who had not yet played; his most inexperienced player. He motioned for the tiny girl at the end of their dugout to grab her bat. The crowd moved to the edge of their seats, some moaning at the decision. Her father, who I think once played pro football, leapt to his feet and clutched the chain-link fence behind home plate as his daughter stepped up to the plate. His huge form eclipsed the batter, catcher, and umpire.

"C'mon, Tiffany, you can do it!" his voice roared, intimidating our players as it could be heard over all the rest of the other fans combined.

As tiny as she was, she mightily swung the giant bat at the first pitch and "clink!" knocked a nice grounder between our first and second basemen. The runner at second was nearly at third when our right-fielder scooped up the ball and threw it to second. Little Tiffany was quick as a bug and easily beat the throw to second for a stand-up double. The second baseman caught the ball and rested her glove on the runner's back.

"*Safe!*" I yelled, holding my hands far out to my sides.

The fans were screaming wildly led by the little girl's mountain of a dad. But before the other runner reached home, Tiffany, shifting her balance, momentarily slid her foot off the bag just an inch, and I could clearly see dirt dividing the two. The glove, with the ball still in it, had never left her back.

"*You're out!*" I shouted instinctively.

"*What!?*" reverberated the dad's voice through the ballpark. "Why you *@#%!" he started screaming and began to climb the fence. Some of the other dads tried to pull him down and cool him off as the umpire faced him through the screen, pointing and yelling at him.

Tiffany looked up at me and calmly said, "You better run."

But I was hot and tired, and I knew what I saw. Thankfully, our second baseman looked Tiffany square in the eyes and said, "You pulled your foot off the bag, and I still had the ball on you."

Just then, the umpire motioned that the overzealous dad "was out of here" and several of the other dads escorted him away from the field.

"I know," said Tiffany. "I better get to him before he gets to you," and she ran to catch up with the men at the field's edge.

The stands calmed down and the game resumed. As it turned out, the other team's rally continued and they easily won the game, negating the value of my call, either way. Little Tiffany, who was the other teams youngest player, was voted MVP for her crucial RBI. Her father was allowed back into the complex to enjoy the impromptu ceremony. I was relieved to see him give me an apologetic nod instead of pulling my arms off and beating me over the head with them.

I was happy to be reassured when things came to a head and temptations may have lead me to make the call I "wanted" rather the one that really "happened"; I had the instinct to make "The Right Call." Oh yeah, and I was ecstatic the season was over!

I Once Had a Boat

The two happiest days in the life of a boat owner is the day they buy the boat and the day they sell it. Most boat owners will agree that the definition of a boat is, "Boat (bōt) > n. A large hole in the water in which one throws money." Knowing this, either by someone warning you, or experiencing it yourself, won't keep you from buying your first or fifth boat.

My first was a beauty; a fire-engine red 16' Critchfield Ski Boat. Her claim to fame was from pulling the shapely young lady skiers at Cypress Gardens in Florida for years. The powerful 150 horse-powered Mercury outboard-motor and tri-pod pulling rig were long gone, but you could still see the scars on her where they'd been. She had since been out-fitted with a 35-hp Evenrude twice her age, but hey, it still ran. I found her behind one of my customer's mill shop where she had been stationed for a half dozen years as a dumpster.

"So," I asked my customer, "How much do you want for the brown boat out back?" I actually didn't discover she was red until I got her home and washed her down.

He reached out and felt my forehead.

"You seem to be well," he said. "Okay, four-hundred dollars and I'll throw in the trailer for free."

Wow! What a bonus! There was so much junk around her that I hadn't noticed she was sitting on a trailer. This was no time for bargaining, others were standing around within earshot and I didn't want this to turn into a bidding war.

"Sold!" I exclaimed.

"You're kidding!" He said.

What a great guy! He said if I paid him cash, he'd let me borrow his pick-up truck to haul it away.

I can't tell you how many looks and smiles I got during the drive back to my place. The pride of boat ownership was overwhelming. I must have worked on her for twelve hours that day. Sure, there were a few things wrong with her; the steering cable was broken, the seats were ripped up, the carpeting was rotted, the gel-coat was gone, there was no gas tank, and the lights and horn didn't work. There were a few more things wrong with the trailer, but when I poured a little gas in the carburetor and pulled the start rope, she'd run for a couple of seconds. And when I found out she was red I actually did a little jig on her bow, spilled some beer on her, and christened her, "Lil' Red."

For several years I spent a great deal of time and a small fortune restoring Lil' Red. Oh, the fun my family and friends had with her. She wasn't the fastest thing on the water. Really, she was about the slowest. But we would take her out and I would pull one of my friends around the lake, and sometimes one of them would actually get up on their skis. A real beauty she turned out to be and everything worked just perfectly. Then one day, just like that, I woke up and the thrill was gone. It was time to sell Lil' Red.

I advertised in the weekend paper and considering everything I invested in her, I had set the price at $1,450. After seven weeks I finally got a call. They were a cute young couple, she was really cute, and they had never owned a boat before. When I opened the garage door and saw their eyes lock on to Lil' Red, I knew I had a sale. They went over her stem to stern, ooing and awing over all they found. They walked off a short distance, conferred with each other for a moment and returned.

"We'll take it," he said. "But the price is a little steep."

I stood frozen, ready not to give an inch. The girl moved a little closer to me. Georgio perfume, I noticed. Very nice. She then reached out and gently touched my arm. I felt my face becoming flush. I was somewhat distracted by her v-neck tank top and mini-shorts. Very revealing. I started to feel a little dizzy. Then, shyly, with a warm wide-eyed smile that was almost teasing, she said, "How about four-fifty?"

My mind drifted a moment fantasizing she was telling me the time and place to meet her for cocktails later on. I don't know where the voice came from, but it was mine.

"Sold!" it said. And before I knew it, she was stuffing a check in my shirt pocket.

"We've never launched a boat before," she said softly, her hand back on my arm. "Is there someplace close you could show us how?"

Still somewhat dazed by the moment, the voice returned. I had no control over it.

"Sure," it said.

There was a little lake with a boat ramp a mile from my house. I pulled the boat with my car, and they followed me with theirs. I launched the boat, speaking out loud all of the steps I was doing as they paid close attention. I was getting ready to reverse the procedure and trailer the thing when she asked coyly, "We've never really been in many boats and never driven any. Would you mind taking us around the lake so we can watch everything you do?"

There was no sense in trying to stop it and I wasn't even shocked when the voice said, "Why not, climb aboard," and off we went.

It was a bright sunny day and the wind felt wonderful rushing past me. It only took a few minutes to circle the lake and as I neared the ramp I looked back at my passengers with their big bright smiles witnessing their pride of boat ownership. So, the voice shouted to them, "Want to go around again?" Yes, they eagerly nodded.

There are two very important aspects of salesmanship at play here. *In sales, when you have the money in your pocket, shake hands with the buyer, thank them, and then move on. Second, if you're going to demonstrate your product, make it short and sweet. The longer you show off, the better chances are something will go wrong.*

Things were going so perfectly when suddenly there was a loud "ba-bump" at the back of the boat. The foot of the motor had struck something large under water. We all spun our heads around to see what had happened. There, in the air, about fifteen up and a dozen yards behind us was the motor. Still running full blast, spinning around like a pinwheel, slinging water and exhaust as it went. Below, all of the cables, tubes, wires, and security chains were flailing wildly out of the back of the boat, like the snakes of Methuselah's head. "Ker-splash!" the motor dove into the lake. In an instant we coasted to a stop and all things were silent except for the popping of the smoky bubbles as they reached the surface where the motor had made its entry.

All transfixed, still looking aft, I thought I heard almost a choking noise coming from the girl. Her hands to her mouth, she turned and faced me. Recognizing her plight, I said, "Go ahead and laugh, honey, you'll never see anything like that again."

Eddie Murphy, in his entire career, never got a laugh so big. She was so weak with laughter that she had to have her companion help out and hand me the paddle that was stowed beside her so that I could row us back to shore. She was able to compose herself enough to ask for the check back. Funny, how quickly someone can lose their cuteness.

When I pulled in the driveway, towing the gutted remains of my maritime pride, my wife was standing there talking to a neighbor. As I got out of the car and tried to slip unnoticed into the house, I heard her say, "Whad-ja-du, lose the motor?"

I stopped, turned, stood erect, and faced the two of them with their arms crossed, poised to give me a scolding on how childish, dangerous, and expensive my hobbies were. This time the voice saved me. It threw them the perfect curve ball that left them bewildered while I made my escape.

It said, "Nope, not at all. I know exactly where it is."

A Post Mortem of Lil' Red

The trio of my boat, motor, and trailer never challenged the waterways again. I sold the trailer to a lawn guy who put a deck on it to carry his mower. The boat was bought by an acquaintance, who threw it in a rental trailer and carried it to Ohio. As fitting a resting place as any, I guess. And two of the guys who worked in my customer's mill shop were amateur divers and recovered the motor. They pulled it up on shore, pulled the start rope, and it ran for a couple of seconds. You gotta love an Evenrude. All in all, I gathered $250 for the remains of Lil'Red, which I promptly traded for a ten-year-old Kawasaki 400 motorcycle. Man, you should have seen my wife's face when I pulled in the garage with that beauty, I mean once the smoke cleared.

Let the Big Dog Eat

"That's just plain nasty," said my wife as I removed the filthy lawn mower bag from the top of a pile of rusty yard equipment in the corner of our garage.

"What are you looking for?" she queried.

"My golf clubs. I thought they were here," I responded.

I continued to dig through the mound of dusty, spider web covered crud.

"Ahh, there they are," I said, spying a tassel from one of the gaudy club covers poking out through the tines of a broken leaf rake.

"But you don't play golf," she said half interested, strapping another kid in a car seat.

"I do tomorrow," I grunted, tugging on the bag's strap in an attempt to wrest it free from the pile.

"I thought you were off tomorrow," her attention completely focused on our conversation, now. "I was going to have you help me take the kids in for their checkup."

"I just said I wasn't making any sales calls tomorrow. The Lumberman's Convention starts tomorrow and I got roped into playing in the golf tournament." I gave another Herculean tug on the strap, and the bag popped loose from the piles grasp and an avalanche of rusty lawn tools, leaves, and dead grass filed the void.

"Harrumph," she anguished as she started the car and backed out of the garage.

Standing at attention, I saluted in her direction and said, "Duty calls, dear," and she drove away.

I actually didn't mind the break from my normal routine, and besides, most of the customers I would usually see tomorrow would be at the golf tournament anyway. With a small whisk broom I swept off the majority of the spider webby, leafy, grassy cocoon that encased the slender bag and threw it in the truck of my car.

I don't really play golf, but they sure charge me as if I do. On top of that, I have to pay them even more for the honor of re-baptizing balls that came from their ponds in the first place. I think I'd rather sit at the bar in the 19th hole, enjoying a cool one, talking to the "bar tendress" about anything, except golf.

I understand most golfers like to get to the course early so they can hit a bucket of balls to loosen up. Not me. I tried that once and left two clubs at the driving range along with my best shots of the day.

It was a "shotgun" start, beginning promptly at seven-thirty in the morning. I got there in plenty of time, I thought, at seven-fifteen. A teenage kid in the county club's uniform was standing on the curb of the parking lot by the "Bag Drop," and I pulled up next to him. He stood at the back of the car while I tried to quickly slip off my tennis shoes and slip on the new black and white saddle Oxford golf shoes I had just purchased at Wal-Mart. I pulled the last Velcro strap tight on them and swung my feet into the parking lot as the kid hollered, "Pop your trunk lid and I'll get your clubs, Sir."

"Okay," I shouted back, as I pushed the release button. "But wait!" I yelled. "The bags top-heavy . . . let me get it!" as I hopped out of the car and started for the rear.

He grabbed the handle on the side of the bag and said, "No problem, sir," and lifted it up. As he cleared the edge of the trunk the lighter bottom of the bag raised faster than the other end and before he could stop it, half my clubs slid out onto the parking lot. To make matters worse, along with the clubs came large clumps of dead grass and leaves and three of the biggest Palmetto bugs I'd ever seen.

"Aawwwk!" the kid screamed as two of the bugs scurried under his feet, and danced to avoid them, screaming the whole time. The remainder of the clubs spilled out along with more landscaping debris and two more bugs. The bugs quickly found safe haven in a perfectly manicured flower garden nearby. The terrified kid just stood there holding the empty bag in the middle of what resembled a Wig-Wam of golf clubs surrounded by an overgrown prairie.

"Well," I finally said. "Looks like you have this under control after all. Don't worry. I'll park my own car." When I was walking back through the lot toward the bag drop, I saw the kid talking to his supervisor while pointing to the compost heap at his feet with one hand and to the flower patch with the other. I slid my sunglasses on and pulled my cap down low. I made a wide detour around them and grabbed my hastily assembled bag from the stand and headed for the starters shack.

"Dahlin! Where the heck have you been?" said my cart-mate as he grabbed my bag and began strapping it to the back of the cart. "Bill's not going to make it and Fred's already at the tee." "Nice set," he continued. "What'd you do, find them on the side of the road?"

Our cart hummed the highest whine it could as we raced past a now empty "sign-in table" and starter's shack and screeched our tires as we skidded up to the 10th Tee. Five other carts waited there as eight colorfully dressed men stood shoulder to shoulder in a line with clubs in their hands at the back of the tee, watching Fred hit away. Our noisy approach turned the heads of them all toward us. My heart rose in my throat as I recognized them. They were the officers, buyers, and top managers of the large home center chain I just started calling on a month earlier.

"Look!" one said as he elbowed the person next to him. "It's Dahlin," he snickered.

"Who?" said the company's president.

"You know," said another, "The guy who lost his motor when he was trying to sell his boat," he laughed.

"Yeah. That's the guy that knocked over the keying kit at Robbie's store," said one of the VP's.

"Oh yeah," nodded the president, and they all laughed simultaneously. "He looks a little green to me. I hope he doesn't hold us up all day."

He was right. I wasn't exactly outfitted as an experienced golfer. I motioned to my partner to go ahead and hit.

"Think man, think!" I said to myself as I instinctively pulled the 3-wood out of my bag. "Wait a minute," I thought. "A long fairway like this? They'll think I'm a sissy if I don't use my driver," I paused. "But I can't hit my driver." I started to panic.

Then it dawned on me. The only way I could lose was to play it safe. I didn't care about the game. All I wanted to do was make a memorable impression on them. A fledgling salesman needs notoriety, even if it's mightily whiffing a tee shot at a golf tournament. Whatever the result was, I simply had to give it my all. I dropped the 3-wood, snatched the "big dog" out of the bag, and put on my best poker face.

"Terrific morning, isn't it!" I announced as I strode in front of them, scratching the face of my driver with the point of a tee, as if I knew what I was doing. Most nodded and a couple continued their snickering. I pushed the tee into the ground with the ball and picked up a pinch of grass, held it in front of me and studied it as I slowly released it from my fingers. I skipped the practice swing and addressed the ball. Everything became silent with the anticipation of the next moment.

My eyes glued to the ball, I started my back swing. "Slow and easy," I thought, "then steady on through the ball." In reality, my backswing was faster than most players forward swing; so much so, the club heads momentum almost caused it to hit me in the left side. It was too late to try to damper the energy wound up in my spring like contortion. I had no alternative but to just let it go. The transfer of power from my body to the club during the down stoke was so intense, my heels popped out of my shoes.

"Sswwooosshh . . . *Clink!*"

"Ahhhh!" I screamed at the ball as it rocketed away. I wasn't attempting to be manly, or anything. My scream was from the pain in the muscles that just tore in my left ribcage. The ball ripped through the dry, cool morning air, arching slightly upward as it shot straight down the fairway. I had never hit a ball that good, before or since.

"Seize the moment," a voice said inside my head. "Finish them off."

I instantly turned and saw their faces with mouths silent and hung open. An assortment of clubs, balls, and tees dropped from their hands as their eyes continued to track the trajectory of my missile. I huffed as I passed them, rubbing imaginary dirt from the big dog's chops and said just loud enough for them to hear, "Crap!" I threw the club in my bag, fell disgustedly in the passenger's seat of the cart and ordered, "Drive . . . just drive!"

My companion, whose mouth also hung open, drove past the group half looking at me and the other half still watching the rolling ball. Their minds couldn't help from formulating the conclusion, "If he didn't like that, what could he really do?" I was happy to have made an impression.

Since my group was a threesome, they never caught up with us the rest of the day. I was glad they didn't as the stabbing pain in my left side prevented me from taking any more full swings. The pain did subside when I received a trophy for the longest ball at the awards lunch that followed. I felt even better when their group brought a beer to me at our table and admired the trophy while chattering about "The Swing."

Life is funny. I've seen many sales reps spend tons of time pulling strings to become acknowledged by this group of guys so they could be invited in their offices for a friendly chat and maybe some business. All I had to do was pull a couple of muscles.

The Six P's

The day had gone smoothly, so far. I had made a couple of sales calls and written some nice orders. This, considering the novice salesman I was, put me in a positive and cheerful mood, which was what I needed as I had arranged a very important sales presentation to take place just after lunch.

"Right after lunch?" Mort said over the phone a week earlier.

"Yeah, the man's visiting his other stores in the morning and is going to meet us at the Prairie Hills store at one-thirty, next Tuesday," I responded. "What's the matter, Mort? 'Fraid you'll miss your nap?" I chided.

Mort, a veteran salesman of some thirty years, was an excellent "cold caller" whom I had worked with on team calls before. He was a talented factory rep and his products were top notch. His charm and charisma always produced positive results and often garnered an order the first time he met a prospective customer.

"I don't know," he stammered. "I like to meet new customers in the morning, you know, when everyone's bright and chipper." Not to overlook the fact that he could usually be found on a golf course most weekday afternoons. "How well do you know this guy?" he added.

Actually, I only met him once at their Annual Contractor's Bar-B-Q and he didn't give me the time of day. He was the son of the owner of the small lumberyard chain and made most of the major buying decisions. I had eked out of the store manager he would be visiting his store that day, and I mentioned to him I would like to talk to them both. In my youthful enthusiasm I figured that constituted a formal appointment and knew if

I could just get Mort in front of them, he could work his magic and we would walk away with an order.

"I've met with him a bunch of times," I lied, "and besides, the store manager will be there and he and I are pals," which we weren't. "And he told me," the lie continued, "if we sold this guy we'd have your line in all four of their stores." I knew I had him with that. No factory rep could resist the potential of writing multiple orders from just one sales call.

"Okay," he finally agreed, "I'll meet you there a little after one."

"Terrific!" I said excitedly. "See you, Tuesday!"

I pulled in the store's parking lot at twelve-thirty. I arrived early so I could check the inventory levels of the products I maintained there and write my restocking order. I also wanted to get my presentation supplies in order for the one-thirty appointment. Haplessly, I accomplished neither.

The retail store wasn't very big, maybe one hundred feet wide and fifty feet deep. But it was packed with gondolas, full of merchandise intermingled with all types of building material displays. The glass and aluminum store front entryway was typical of an establishment that size. The bright early afternoon sun had passed its zenith and flooded the first three or four feet inside the store with light.

I awkwardly managed to pull open the glass door with the hand clinging to the leather handles of my thirty-five-pound catalog as my other arm was wrapped around a large window sample, brochures, and order pad. Making it though the doorway intact was an admirable feat, and I stood on the sunlit welcome mat a moment to let my eyes adjust to the store's lighting before I resumed my entrance. The retail sales counter was less than ten feet away, directly in front of me, where two cashiers were busy checking out a line of eight or nine customers. I nodded and smiled at the group en total and decided my vision was sufficient to continue.

Just then the sample shifted under my arm to an unstable position, and I was in danger of losing it. Quickly, I spotted a space to drop my catalog so that the freed hand could stabilize the juggling act going on in the other. The catalog's drop zone was next to a large cylindrical ash tray about two feet tall and a foot in diameter. Its top was filled with sand, peppered with cigarette butts. Some knucklehead had cruelly left a very large, three-quarter-full fountain drink, cap and straw in place, stuffed in the sand and butt mixture. Gracelessly, I release the big book and unsuccessfully tried to stabilize the contents of my other arm.

"Crash!" the sample hit the floor, shattering the glass. The crowd at the sales counter swung their heads in my direction. Sadly, one of the falling catalog handles swayed outward further than I had anticipated and snagged the straw protruding from the gigantic cup, pulling it downward. The weight was too much for the top-heavy ashtray to handle and resembling an abstract sculpture, teetered like the Leaning Tower of Pizza. I made a spastic move to catch it but bumped the base of it with my foot and the whole thing fell over on the slick linoleum floor casting sand and butts all the way to feet of the stunned customers. A moment passed and I thought the worst was over when the cup, now laying on its side in the gritty compost, popped its top and a pint and a half of sticky-sweet liquid washed through the sandy feet of the helpless observers.

I felt as if I were on a spot-lit stage as their gaze moved from their sticky, sandy feet to me. All I could do was to open my empty arms out wide and with a sheepish grin, said, "Ta-dah!" One guy gave me a small round of applause and I nodded meekly in his direction.

The clean-up routine took a full forty-five minutes, consisted of me pushing a broom and mop interspersed with apologizes to everyone. I was almost finished picking up the last few soggy butts on my hands and knees when I heard a familiar voice over me.

"What the heck are you doing down there?" I looked up. It was Mort.

"Oh, just helping out, where I can," I said with the sheepish grin that had become my permanent expression.

I stood up, brushing off my pants and started to fabricate a much less embarrassing account of the previous hour's experience when I saw our appointment walking in the contractor's entrance at the side of the store.

"There they are," I interrupted myself. "You ready?"

We sauntered up to them as the manager was unlocking his office door.

"Hi, Carey," I announced, offering my handshake to the manager, as his companion checked the math from his lunch receipt and succumbed to a major yawn.

"Oh . . . Dale, how's it goin'," Carey said, unenthusiastically.

"I guess you guys are ready for our big meeting!" I offered optimistically.

"Meeting?" Carey said queerly. "Not me. I have a dentist's appointment. I'm just letting Craig in to use my office." I could feel Mort's eyes starting to glare at me.

"Oh, well then, we'll just have to have our meeting with Craig, alone," turning my attention to the owner's son.

"Hi. I'm Dale Dahlin. We've met several times before," I said, offering him my still unshaken hand.

Folding the receipt and stuffing it in his shirt pocket, he stifled another yawn and said, "Who?"

Mort shot a look in my direction that instantly chastised me for not only leading him into an afternoon cold call, but also for doing a miserable job of preparing the customer for our meeting.

Keys still in his hand, Carey made a half-hearted apology and added, "If he wants to meet with you guys, it's okay by me," and left for his appointment.

Craig said, "Sure," yawning as he walked into the office.

I motioned Mort to follow him but he turned to me and said in a low voice, "I'm going to let you slide on this one, pal. You just sit there and take my cues. I'm going to do my best to put this fella to sleep. He doesn't know you from Adam and I don't want him to remember me either. I'm not going to waste my first impression on this guy, this way." We walked in the office and quietly sat in the two chairs facing the semi-conscious man slumped behind the desk. I watched the master go to work.

Mort never cracked a smile or told a joke. His voice was monotone and with every sentence I could see Craig sinking further in his chair. When I tried to offer him one of my sticky brochures and broken sample, Mort deftly took them from me and set them on the floor between us. Instead he handed him some innocuous government report and recited figures from the many graphs and charts, all the time his voice getting softer. I must admit, I started feeling sleepy as I watched Craig's eyelids get heavier and heavier. Finally, Mort gently touched my arm, which startled me a little as I was beginning to doze.

"Let's go," he whispered. "He's out." We studied Craig, who was breathing slowly with eyes shut tight, still holding the report with both hands resting on the desk. "Get the sample and brochure," he motioned to the floor. "And don't forget our calling cards."

"What about the report?" I whispered back.

"I have plenty of those and besides, it doesn't have my name on it." We eased out of the room and silently closed the door.

"Sorry, Mort," I said as we stepped out of the store.

"That's all right, kid. It happens. What was that gooey stuff all over the brochures?" he asked.

"Just more of what had to be the worst sales call ever," I said humbly.

"Yeah," he said consolingly. "Listen, kid, I saw a driving range a couple of miles down the road. Want to share a bucket or two? I have my clubs in the trunk."

"Naw, thanks anyway," as I shook my head. I wasn't about to add playing hooky to my list of failures that day.

We spit a six-pack as we stood in the tee boxes at the range, sharing stories and smacking golf balls the rest of the afternoon. I picked up a bunch of handy sales techniques, one of them being to never make a cold call after lunch. The most important though was the lesson about "The Six P's." **P**oor **P**lanning **P**rovides for **P**iss **P**oor **P**erformance. I will never forget it and that day.

A footnote to this story is Craig never remembered our meeting or at least didn't tell anyone about it. And, Mort was successful in getting his line of goods in all four of their locations. I just wish he would have invited me to go along with him on that call.

Now, with Feeling

I was an outside salesman for a building material wholesaler in Florida. I had been there for about ten years and had made many lifelong friends. Fellow salesmen Greg and Bobby were, and still are, two of my favorites. Kind of a Laurel and Hardy team, with Bobby being somewhat better looking than Laurel and Greg being more deviant than Hardy; their antics and practical jokes on each other, at the dismay of management, kept the rest of us in stiches.

Once a month the company would bring together all of our sales reps from Florida and Georgia to our home office for a Friday night dinner meeting where we would discuss internal business and a Saturday morning meeting where vendors would come in and show us what was new with their product lines. All of us were definitely unique in personality and appearance. We had everything from city slickers to country bumpkins, and since I didn't speak Spanish, I never knew what to think about the guys from Miami. Everyone said we had a lot of class; unfortunately most of it was low.

Marvin, our Sales Promotion Manager, was the fellow who put together the agenda for the meetings, presided over them, and also made the dinner and lodging arrangements. To say Marvin was tight was an understatement, which delighted the two elderly brothers who ran the business as General Manager and Sales Manager. They were just plain cheap.

Marvin, on the other hand, was our saving grace at any attempt of dignity. Somewhat resembling Marlin Brando's elderly godfather character, without the gauze-stuffed cheeks, Marvin was well dressed, poised, organized, well spoken, but kind of had a vindictive mean streak at times and could have been mislabeled as a stuffed shirt. But since he had a good sense of humor and possessed many of the necessary traits the brothers lacked, he was an intricate component of the company's success.

The vindictive side became apparent to me when I enquired of a fellow salesman why we stayed at such a cheap hotel and why we had our morning meeting in a cramp little room in the corner of the second floor of one of our warehouses.

"It wasn't always that way," he said. "We used to stay at different hotels in the area and use their nice meeting facilities to hold our meetings. A couple of times the guys would get a little rowdy in the hotel lounge after the Friday night meeting. And sometimes we would leave the rooms a little messier than we should have. But the final straw came when one of our vendors invited us to his beautiful home in the suburbs for a cook out and informal Friday night meeting. It was an open bar, and well, one thing led to another, and half the salesmen ended up in the pool with their clothes on along with most of the living room furniture. From then on we've been meeting in the Downtown Daze Inn."

"Did the salesmen always have to share rooms?" I enquired.

"Nope. That's just Marvin getting back at us for embarrassing him."

This was no inconvenience for Marvin or the two brothers as they lived close by and didn't have to stay at the fleabag hotel. But, this did leave all of the salesmen unsupervised after the meeting, which occasionally meant someone getting tossed in the pool. Sometimes it was one of our guys and sometimes we'd throw in a complete stranger. I guess we were just fascinated by swimming pools.

Marvin was a great planner and could manipulate a meeting's content and duration at will. Sometimes he would drag out the Friday night meeting until midnight knowing that the hotel bar shut down at 1:30 a.m. He knew that he would have mostly non-hung-over salesmen in the morning meeting. Sometimes he was just disgusted with us from the previous month's meeting and ended things early so that he could simply get away from us. This was the case for this particular meeting.

You see, at the previous month's Saturday morning meeting, Bobby, sometimes referred to as Cheetah (as in Tarzan's chimp), found a really big rubber band in one of the warehouse trash cans and put it in his shirt pocket. Everyone filed in the side door of the 10' by 30' room and took their seats around the long Formica meeting table. About twenty salesmen and buyers sat at this table with the end left open for the vendor to make their presentation. Marvin and the two brothers always sat in the first three seats next to the presenter. There was no other assigned seating so when Bobby came in, he took a seat closest to the door and immediately took out the rubber band and started playing with it. He was pretending to shoot people with it just to be annoying, yet he was careful none of the bosses saw his new toy. When Greg entered the room, Bobby was stretching it out as if he were going to shoot the elderly salesmen sitting next to him. Seeing this, as he walked by, Greg plucked the rubber band from Bobby's fingers and went for the open seat furthest from the vendor and the bosses.

Bobby jumped up in protest and started for Greg when Marvin said, "Let's get things started. Bobby, sit down."

Bobby stood there defiantly, starring at Greg who was dangling the prize from his finger.

"Bobby," Marvin said again and then the younger brother, Buck, snapped, "Cheetah, sit!"

The vendor started his presentation and all eyes were on him, except for Bobby who silently mouthed back at Greg, "Gimmie back my rubber band."

When Bobby turned his head forward, Greg deftly stretched the thing back as far as he could and shot it at Bobby's head. It was one of those moments that you could practice forever but never reproduce the exact timing. While the projectile was in the air, Bobby glanced back at Greg. Seeing the object flying at his face he instinctively jerked his head back. Marvin was looking down at his notes and then looked back to the salesmen to see if all were paying attention.

Smack! The rubber band hit Marvin right in the forehead and hung from his glasses. He gave out a little gasp. He still didn't know what hit him; the thing continued to just hang there. The rest of the salesmen were quite used to things like this and didn't move a muscle. Bobby and Greg gave the look of being perfect attentive angels. The vendor, who observed the entire incident, gave out a larger gasp as his gaze was fixed on Marvin.

The brothers followed his gaze to Marvin, and then Hobart, the elder of the two, said to his brother, "Isn't he a little old to be playing with rubber bands?"

Buck reached over and seized the object of much distraction from Marvin's glasses and put it in his own pocket, turned back to vendor and said, "My apologies, he's usually more in control of himself. Please continue."

Needless to say, Marvin was absolutely infuriated and turned more shades of crimson than basket of fall persimmons. Twenty years later, even after the passing of the brothers, we still haven't told him who fired the shot.

This month's Friday night meeting started as usual with the serving of the mystery beast. We all guessed if it was meatloaf, Salisbury steak, or just plain hamburger.

"North Atlantic grilled Salmon," interjected the waiter.

Twenty-three plates of food were either pushed away or covered with a napkin. Marvin ate every last bite of his.

After the dishes were cleared, Marvin would start the meeting by going through all of the typical sales reports, every month the same reports in the same order. Then he would turn things over to Hobart, who would say three sentences about preserving profits, reducing returns, and collecting money, and then leave immediately after he was finished. After all, where does an 800-pound gorilla sit, certainly not in the Downtown Daze Inn? Then Buck would light up a fat cigar, lean back in his chair, and compare some of our salesmen to a monkey doing something with a football or a chimpanzee riding a motor scooter. I really never understood what he was talking about, but I think he had a thing for apes. Then Marvin would take over again and sometimes go on for hours. We hoped it was going to be a short meeting this month because of the previous month's incident. And just to insure things, at a prescribed moment, all of the salesmen reached in their shirt pockets and pulled out a really big rubber band and started playing with them.

Seeing this, Marvin slumped back in his chair, parted his hands, looked at Buck and said, "How am I supposed to do anything with them?"

Buck pulled out a rubber band from his pocket and stuck it between his forehead and glasses, and while jiggling his head to make the thing wiggle, said, "Golly, Marvin, I thought you like playing with these things."

"Goodnight," Marvin said as he folded up his notebook and headed for the door.

"To the bar," Buck saluted Marvin's empty seat beside him with an empty glass.

"To the bar," we all echoed in the same manner.

The rest of the evening went on as it had done dozens of times before. Everyone would jostle for position to hang around Buck at the bar, after about three rounds he would head for the restroom and never come back. We knew he had enough and had gone home.

Then we would watch a sports game on the TV above the bar; someone would get in an argument with someone else and then "Splash" in the pool they'd go.

The bar closed at the usual time and everyone helped everyone else get up to their rooms for hopefully an uneventful night of unconsciousness. As wise as pairing a gallon of nitro-glycerin and a paint shaker, Marvin had arranged for Greg and Bobby to be in the same room. As fate would have it, at this monument of hotel hopelessness, some late night returning partying patron tried to steady himself while unlocking his door by hanging on the fire alarm pad with his free hand and oops, the fire alarm was activated on all six floors.

Always hyper and nervous as a cat, Bobby sprung from his bed the instant the alarm sounded. Wearing only his leopard skin speedo style underwear, supposedly fashionable at that time, he raced to the door and glued his eye to the peephole. From the darkness behind him Greg asked what could he see.

"Nothin'," said Bobby. "Everything looks fine. I don't see nothin'."

The alarm still blaring, Greg urged, "Well, why don't you poke your head out and take a look down the hallway?"

Bobby opened the door a little and stuck his head out. Like most hotel hallways, the room entrances were recessed about a foot in from the hall and really didn't give Bobby a view at the end.

"You can't see anything from there. Go out and take a good look," directed Greg.

"Okay," said Bobby.

No sooner than he had swung the door open enough to go out, Greg's hand was on Bobby's back and shoved him completely out into the hallway and then slammed the door behind him.

Stunned for a moment, standing there in the middle of the hall in all of his near nakedness, save for the leopard skin underwear, which now seemed way too small, Bobby turned and leapt back at the door.

"You let me in, Greg! You let me in or so help me . . . !"

"You look real threatening out there in your underpants," said Greg as he spied through the peephole. "I don't know if it would be safe to let you in. You should calm down," he instructed.

"People are starting to come out of their rooms, Greg," Bobby said as he attempted to press himself flat out of view in to the door alcove. "Let me in now!"

"You know what calms people down? Singing songs. That calms them down alright," Greg droned on. "Why don't you sing me a song?"

Bobby froze, partly because he was trying to become invisible by becoming a plank in the door and partly because he was using all of his mental powers to try and figure his way out of this predicament. "What kind of song," he said as now more than a dozen people were in the hallway, staring at him.

Greg thought for a moment, "How about the Star Spangled Banner?"

Having no choice, Bobby started out in almost a whisper.

"No, no!" said Greg. "Sing it proudly, sing it loudly, and back up if you want to get in."

Bobby's facial expression, one of mixed anger and terror, and the ridged-ness of his body still pressed against the door, both went limp in surrender. He backed up to the middle of the hall and began, "Oh-oh, say can you see . . ."

About three quarters of the way through his performance the alarm stopped. He stopped also and stared at the door's peephole.

"Strong finish" came from the other side. "Let's have a strong finish, now with feeling."

So he did. And what a beautiful rendition it was. Respectfully and somewhat entranced, the onlookers gave him a nice round of applause. On guy said, "Play ball" and then they all retired to their rooms.

Finally, the door slowly opened. Too exhausted to retaliate, Bobby dragged himself back into the room and slumped into bed.

"Someday, Greg," Bobby murmured. "Someday I'll get even." And he was right. There were many more "some days" for them both yet to come.

Friends . . . good friends, enjoy embarrassing or playing jokes on each other. It's a sort of camaraderie thing or team-building exercise, if you will. If you're part of a sales team, don't miss out on the fun. Don't be a wall flower at sales meetings and functions. Jump in, get in the spirit of things, you don't have to throw anyone in the pool. But if you happen to get tossed in, don't lose your cool. Learn to handle these moments gracefully. It is terrific practice for those unpredictable embarrassing situations that happen when making a presentation to a customer.

Bon Appetite

"I got him!" Lonnie blurted as he stumbled though the small office's doorway and fell into the old arm chair in the corner. Tears streamed down the red cheeks of his broad face as one hand pressed against his large belly and the other cupped his brow and eyes in a futile attempt to bring his explosive fit of laughter under control. Robbie, startled from the unexpected intrusion, looked up quickly from the myriad of meticulously positioned reports on the large desk that occupied nearly half of the tiny office.

"Got who?" he returned, in a somewhat stunned and slightly annoyed voice.

Lonnie tried to compose himself by leaning forward, stretching his arms out with fingers open and palms facing down, as if he was trying to keep something big from floating away.

"Okay . . . I'm okay, now," he said, trying to restrain his laughter.

"Got who?!" Robbie demanded.

Lonnie's lips pressed together in a painful grin, his eyes squinted and more tears rolled down his face. He looked as if he was going to pop, when he choked out, "I don't know!" He totally lost control and fell to his hands and knees on the floor, whooping with laughter so loudly it could be heard throughout the entire store.

Robbie's annoyance faded away and was replaced with amusement at his longtime friend and coworker's pitiful condition. Still completely in the dark as to the nature of Lonnie's triumphant declaration, he couldn't help from joining him in his laughter.

It felt good to laugh this rainy Friday afternoon, as the entire week had been a very trying one for Robbie, who managed a location in a fifteen-unit retail building materials chain. It was the end of the month and all of the various reports regarding lumber sales, truss production projections, inventory status, and employee issues were to be completed by the end of the day. The sales for his store were the highest in the company and his roof-truss plant's production was the best it had ever been. All would have been terrific except trouble was brewing in the truss plant and he was in jeopardy of losing his high production rate over a simple employee issue. Someone had been stealing lunches from the refrigerator in the truss plant break room. A problem like this might seem trite to some, but in the environment of a truss plant, it can be deadly.

Most of the workers there made only minimum wage, with little overtime pay. Not only was the cost of a lunch a significant percentage of their daily income, it also was the main source of energy to keep the workers focused on their duties in the physically demanding and dangerous surroundings of a large manufacturing facility. Angry, grumbling stomachs can lead to conflicts between suspicious workers, and several fights had already broken out. And that can be devastating to a production schedule.

Robbie had done his best to deal with the matter. In early morning meetings with workers, he had instructed everyone to put their name on their lunch bag. Lunch boxes, while looking unique, were prohibited as they took up too much room in the refrigerator. Everyone was forced to pack their lunches in brown paper bags. He also informed them when the lunch thief was caught, he would be immediately fired and then turned over to the police. Since most of the workers didn't speak English, he had the company's bi-lingual HR Manager interpret his remarks. Every day that week one or more upset workers came to his office at lunch time to complain. Not understanding a word they said, he knew what they were angry about. But today was different. Lunchtime had come and gone and no one had come into his office, except Lonnie, who was the plant supervisor.

Robbie's eyes too were wet from laughter now and he dabbed them with a paper napkin left over from his own lunch. Lonnie's convulsive fits subsided and he gathered enough strength again to sit back in the chair.

"I'm sorry, boss," he said, still chuckling. "But I had to take matters in my own hand. I got the lunch thief," he said proudly.

"Well, where is he? Who is it?" Robbie questioned.

"I don't know where or who he is, but I can tell you this," he continued. "He won't be stealing lunches anymore."

Robbie, tired of asking the same question, tilted his head to the side and said flatly, "I'm listening."

"Well," Lonnie started, "when you told everyone to put their name on their lunch bag, it got me thinking. This guy's getting pretty gutsy and I think he's starting to do this for the thrill of it, too. So, this morning I asked my wife to make me a nice big meat loaf sandwich with lettuce, tomatoes, pickles, and everything," he continued. "She folded it neatly in waxed paper and put it in a brown bag with *my* name on it. I got to work this morning and stuffed it in the truss fridge with the other lunches."

"So," still trying to figure things out, Robbie stated, "You got him . . . but you didn't catch him?"

"Hold on now," Lonnie went on. "So I checked the fridge after lunch and my bag was the only one left."

"Okay, now I'm really confused," said Robbie.

Starting to laugh again, Lonnie said, "So, I got on the truss plant PA system and announced in Spanish and English that the 'lunch thief had been caught.'"

"But, but . . . your lunch was still there?" said Robbie, screwing up his face.

"I know, I know," Lonnie cackled. "This had to drive the thief crazy."

Robbie quit attempting to understand anything and just sat there with his mouth gaping open.

"So, I waited an hour and just went out there again and the bag was gone," laughing more steadily now.

"But you didn't see who took it," Robbie was shaking his head, his mouth still open.

"No . . . no, I didn't," composing himself the best he could. "But I walked around the corner and I saw my bag on the ground, then the waxed paper, and then the sandwich . . . with a big bite out of it!"

"So the guy doesn't like meat loaf. So what?" Robbie said, still shaking his head.

"*No!* That's not it!" he chortled, trying to suppress his laughter. Ya see, I had taken the meatloaf off and replaced it with a "Bubba-pie."

"Bubba-pie?" Robbie repeated.

"Yeah . . . you know, Bubba's my dog, you know, dog poop!" he exclaimed. "Like I said, boss, I don't know who the son-of-a-gun is . . . but I got him!"

Robbie leaned back in his chair and belted out the biggest laugh he had in years.

Fortunately, the lunch stealing ended that day. The fighting stopped. Truss plant production kept up with its forecast, and the HR department never heard any more of the distasteful event. All because an ingenious supervisor took matters into his own hands and solved the problem.

Two weeks later Robbie summoned Lonnie to his office.

"Well, pal," he started, "we have a new problem. Someone is stealing the toilet paper out of the truss plant bathroom and the other workers are complaining about it."

Without pausing a moment Lonnie smiled and said, "Not to worry about it, boss, I'll take care of it."

And he did.

Things Are
Looking Up—Not Good

The skill of selling can be a peculiar talent. If often takes years of practice and experimentation in this trade to acquire the skills to influence someone to do something they wouldn't ordinarily do. To have a customer confide their trust in you and buy something from you based solely on the presentation you make them is the pinnacle of sales achievement. Once acquired, this talent is a formidable tool and must be applied with great care, just as a surgeon does with his scalpel. We've all heard the saying, "The operation was a great success, but the patient died anyway." Sometimes a successful sale can be disastrous.

Ceiling fans were not always the commodity they are today. Back in the 1980s, there were only a few steadfast, high-quality, and high-priced brands to choose from. The fans were rarely found in anything except fancy restaurants and expensive custom homes. The American home building industry was on an upward swing and builders and home-owners demanded new products in their homes. Overnight, multitudes of ceiling fan manufacturers were on the scene and competition became fierce. As it happened, one of the major manufacturers I represented developed a line of ceiling fans and hastily packaged it for distribution. After our sales team was given a full-blown presentation of the line (although no fans were actually turned on), our management dictated we must capture our share of the rapidly growing ceiling fan market and marched us out to accomplish our goal. Armed with brochures, price lists, and a sample fan blade, white on one side and wood-grain on the other, I immediately set out to make the first sale for the company.

Jerry was the manager of my largest account and we had become good friends and confidants.

"Do I have something for you!" I exclaimed as I burst into his office. "You're going to remember this day proudly, as the day you made the decision to take on the most cutting-edge brand of ceiling fan technology," as I handed him the fan blade and a brochure.

I hardly let him get a word edgewise as I mimicked our ceiling fan display and his customers entranced by them. I pranced around his office, answering all of his questions before he could ask them. The skill of my presentation electrified the room and enthralled his co-workers who poked their heads in his office to see what all the commotion was about.

"You're really charged up about this, aren't you," he said, still holding the blade and brochure.

"I tell you, Jerry, this is the greatest thing I've ever seen," I boasted.

"Alright," he mused, "Give me the 'A' assortment and the big display. And, oh yeah, send an extra ten 'El Presidenté' models. The owner of the company is just finishing his new home and he wants a ceiling fan in every room. I'll have to cancel the other ones I have on order and hate doing that to somebody. But you've convinced me."

Wow! I was so excited I forgot to get my sample blade back from him and drove twenty miles to my office to personally write up the order. When I finished it, I paraded it to the sales manager's office and proudly laid it on his desk.

He called in his assistant and said, "Have the switchboard operator tell all the salesmen as they call in, that Dahlin got the first ceiling fan order and influenced his customer to cancel an order with our competitor, to boot!" I was big man on campus for some time after that. A couple of weeks went by and the fans were finally delivered to my customer, and I happily set up the display and stocked his shelves with my product.

On my next visit to Jerry I discovered that he was at a job site and wanted to meet me there. The job site was the owner's new home. "Great," I thought. "I hope I have enough film in my Polaroid so I can show off the pictures of my installed fans at our next sales meeting."

I'd been to the house several times before during construction, but was awed by the magnificence of its finished state as I drove through the large iron gates and into the circular driveway. As I got out of my car, I thought it strange I could hear what seemed to be several orbital sanders grinding inside the house. The house had been finished for weeks except for a few lighting fixtures and my fans, which were to have been installed yesterday. I rang the doorbell but had to resort to use the oversized door knocker to get any response. The massive front door was opened by Tommy, the owner, who stood in the doorway with sort of a dazed look on his face.

"Hi, Tommy!" I shouted as the sanding noise was much louder now.

"What!" he shouted back. I could see over his shoulder Jerry was in the formal living room, looking up. Because the loud grinding noise made conversation pointless, Tommy motioned me in.

"Love your new house!" I shouted.

He held up his hand to stop me from trying to continue and turned off a switch on the wall next to him. The grinding noise stopped, well at least in the living room. I could still hear it in other rooms throughout the house. The fan above Jerry's head began to slow just as Tommy's usually pleasant wife rounded the corner of the hallway saying, "Is he here, yet? This noise is driving me crazy!" She then noticed me standing on the other side of Tommy and just folded her arms and stared at me.

"Uh-oh," I said softly.

Just then, there was the sound of breaking glass coming from the great room.

"What's that?" I questioned, excitedly.

"It's another light bulb vibrating out of one of your ceiling fans," she said as a matter of fact, while piercing me with a squinted stare. "I think if we left them on for an hour, they'd all fall out."

Jerry lowered his head and looked at me as the fan above his head ground to a halt. "Well?" he said.

I assured them I would take care of the problem and could we please turn these things off before somebody gets hurt.

"Well?" I said to my sales manager after reciting the events of the day and laying ten Polaroid photos on his desk. That "Well" went back to the manufacturer and several more times up their corporate ladder. As a result, the "El Presidenté" was recalled and the customers were refunded. Our competitor got his order after all and we installed his fans at our expense.

My customer's trust in me was restored and an important lesson for the talented sales person should be learned from my experience. **"Don't be so cocksure about a product until you've tried it. Your reputation is far more valuable than one sale."** And believe me; you don't want to hear this quipped at you after your next presentation, "This isn't going to be like the ceiling fans, is it?"

The Naked Stairway

In selling, I have always found the more you know about your products, the more opportunities you'll have to sell them. The company I worked for had many product lines. Some were easy to learn and some were difficult and required extensive training to become proficient. Selling stair systems was one of the latter. If you studied hard and learned this product line well, pricing became a non-issue and your customers would demand that you sell them your product. Making an accurate stair parts take-off and quotation for a builder or owner builder should not be tackled by an amateur. It takes experience and a keen eye to ensure customer satisfaction. Well, most of the time, anyway.

I arrived at my customer's place of business early that sunny spring afternoon. There was a note for me from the manager pinned to the vendor's bulletin board. It said he was on vacation that week and could I please do a job site, stair take off for him and go ahead and order it. It also left the home owner's name and phone number. I called them, now was a good time for them, they said, and gave me the directions to their home. South about a mile to the stop light, then right, and right at the stop sign, then left to the guard house. The directions sounded familiar and I thought I must have driven by it a hundred times, but I just couldn't think of the community's name.

I remembered it well enough when I pulled up to the guard house. It was Paradise Hills, a nudist community. I'm a professional and I wanted my customer to be able to count on me. Nakedness or not, I was going to complete my task.

The gate guard laughed and told me I didn't have to take off my clothes, too. He said that during the weekdays most of the residents were at work and most of the rest were clothed. I gave him the name of the people who were expecting me and he gave me a little map showing the way to their condo. He also told me when I was talking to them I should speak up a little as they were the oldest residents in the community and a bit hard of hearing.

I was consumed with nightmarish visions of two ancient naked bodies covered in wrinkles trying to get closer to hear me as I, in horror, vainly tried to utter my introduction. With a shaking hand, I rang the doorbell. They answered the door fully clothed. Both were in their eighties and appeared to be your typical well-to-do retired couple. My sigh of relief was so audible the old lady asked if I was all right. After I composed myself, they let me in and introductions were made. The old lady brought me a glass of iced tea as the old man and I stood gazing at the large circular stairway in the middle of their entry hall.

"It just looks old. We want something more contemporary, with perkiness; you know . . . something with bounce. Money is no object," he said, while she nodded. "Come, Mother, let's sit and see what this young man can do for our stairs. He's highly recommended, you know."

They led me into a rather large formal living room with a great picture window at the end and two overstuffed chairs on either side of it, facing the center of the room. They seated themselves and motioned me to stand in front of them.

My selling cap on, I took center stage and began my presentation. I passed over my introduction where I explain the meaning of the word *stairway* and tell them of the ancient civilization who invented stairs, fearing that these people may have personally known them and challenge me on technical point. I handed them each a piece of literature full of pictures of beautiful stairways. It was then I noticed through the oversized picture window that I was not more than a dozen feet away from the tennis courts directly in front of me. Well, there was a walkway, and a six-foot-strip of grass and then the chain-link fence surrounding the courts. And, oh my, there were naked people playing tennis. Mixed pairs. I mean the players, that is.

But, I'm a professional. I stayed focused on the sale and not on the game or the participants, who appeared to be young, well formed, and nicely tanned so early in the season. I was just explaining the entasis of a perfectly shaped set of circular stairs when she appeared. I had successfully completed so many stair jobs with unbelievable distractions that I had no doubt I would come through this one with flying colors. I was wrong.

In her late twenties, maybe early thirties she was. Slender yet curvy with long blonde hair pinned up in a little poof above her head, wrap-around sunglasses, a flawless golden tan complexion, with ruby red lips. She was wearing some sort of a swim suit cover-up, with a fold out chair under one arm and a bottle of tanning lotion in her free hand. She strode down the far side of the court, some distance away, and then out of sight as she passed out of my field of view to the left side of the window. "Walk on" I thought and continued with my explanation of the importance of selecting proper balusters and newels.

I stuttered the moment she came in to view again from the left, this time on this side of the court, on the walkway directly in front of the old couple's window. "Don't stop, don't stop," I thought. "Drat!" Right in front of the picture window, she stopped. While she paused, she looked left at the grassy strip this side of the tennis courts. "No, no!" I screamed inside my head. "I can't be distracted. I have a sale to make." The grassy area was slightly sloped downhill to me and the way the sun was shining did make for an excellent sunning spot.

"Treads, risers, hand rails, all very important choices," I said aloud to the couple. They were still seemingly enthralled with the pictures of the stairs and hadn't yet noticed that I had become captivated with something quite different.

The young lady opened the lounge chair on the grassy strip and faced it at about a forty-five percent angle toward me. She sat in it, and while still robed, put some lotion on her fingertips and began smoothing it on her face. "Ah, just out to get some face tanning I bet." Wrong again. She then untied the sash of her robe, pulled her arms from the sleeves, laid the robe open and showed to the sun and me her complete form, unencumbered. She reached for the lotion.

"No! No! Stop!" I said to myself, or at least I thought.

"What?" said the old man.

She started with her shoulders, then her arms and then her . . .

"Stop! Not there!" I said.

"We're not following you." He said.

"Not the other one!" I blurted.

"Who the hell is he talking to?" said the old lady.

Then they leaned forward and turned to the window. "Gwen!" they said in unison. They turned back in their chairs and looked at the Picasso that was my face.

"Oh, that's just great, Father. We've lost another one."

"Third salesman this week. I don't think we'll ever get new stairs. You know, Mother, I think she does this on purpose."

Still trembling, I found myself in my car in the parking lot. My brochures gone and my order pad empty. It just goes to show, no matter how professional and trained you are, you just can't prepare for everything.

A Time to Pass

A long-time friend who was a customer and eventually a coworker passed away the day before yesterday, which brought to mind a past experience . . .

In the life of a traveling salesman you meet a lot of people and if you enjoy what you do, you make a lot of friends. As a territorial salesman I called on most of my accounts once a week. That's just enough time for events to happen regarding family, friends, business, and the world at large, giving plenty of topics to discuss and stories to trade with all of my customer friends. It is truly as wonderful life and the good experiences out-weigh the bad, one hundred to one. The worst of the bad is when one of them passes away.

Most folks can handle the funerals and visitations in stoic stride. They can say a few consoling words to those who need them, sit respectfully, and leave quietly. Others may shed a tear and occasionally weep softly. But not me, I turn into a blubbering spectacle, barely able to breathe, much less able to offer sympathetic words, gasping for air between long stretches of out-and-out bawling. Incapable of standing, I have to wait for someone to help me up and out of the room so that others can carry on with their respects for the deceased. To say the least, as much as I love my friends, I dread going to their funerals. My trepidation for funerals is so strong I don't plan on going to my own.

One of my accounts was a classic, old-style, out-in-the-country lumber yard. The main building housed a small retail store and paint counter with a long sales counter at the end where three or four sales clerks were stationed. In a windowed room to the side was the manager's office and a little further down was the contractor's sales office. It was an open and friendly place where you could stand at the sales counter and literally see everyone at once. Since I had become friends with everyone there, I could walk behind the counter and in and out of offices as I chose. I was made to feel as if I were at home.

One of the countermen was an elderly fellow who out-ranked me by thirty years. Even with our age difference, we were able to become friends and enjoyed trading stories with each other. I was dismayed, but not shocked, when one of the other countermen called me one day and informed me the old fella's recent illness had taken a turn for the worse. He passed a few days later. I called the store to get the information on the arrangements that had been made. My intention was to just go to the visitation and pay my respects and not to attend the funeral. It was to be a full Catholic Mass and funeral about two hours long. I tried to endure one of those before. Thankfully, a couple of ushers helped me out to the parking lot early on so the service could continue.

My sense of direction is so bad I used to get lost on my own farm. They would have to send the dogs out to find me and drag me back to dinner. I followed the driving instructions I was given, and as usual, had to back track several times before I located the funeral home and parked my car. My knees started shaking, eyes started to water, and the old familiar lump in my throat made speech impossible, and I wasn't but half way through the parking lot.

It was a small funeral chapel and there were only two visitation rooms with a nice elderly lady sitting at a receptionist's desk between them. Wanting to avoid any attempt at conversation, I headed for the room on the left.

"Sir?" she said kindly, "That room is empty. Who are you here to see?"

I tried to utter his name, but nothing came out.

"A family member?" she said, recognizing I was unable to speak.

I shook my head, "No."

"A friend, then?" she continued.

"Yes," I nodded.

"A very old friend?" she went on.

My knees were starting to give way and tears streamed down my face. I steadied myself with my hands on her desk and nodded profusely.

"Oh, poor child," she said consolingly. "Let me help you into the chapel."

She got up and came around the desk. Feeble as she may have appeared, when she took me by the arm with one hand and the other around my waist, it felt as if two sturdy Coast Guardsmen were lifting me out of a sinking boat. As she capably led me into the room I tried to focus on the little stand by the door with the names of the deceased and family members on it, as I wanted to refresh my memory of everyone's name. But, my eyes were so full of tears I couldn't make out anything. I nodded to a large couch against the back wall. She helped me sit on the middle cushion and handed me a box of tissues from a nearby table.

"Will you be all right, dear?" she asked quietly, while patting my hand.

"A simple yes," I thought I could utter. Instead what came out was a loud "sob" as I gasped for air.

There weren't many people in the room, as the actual starting time had yet to arrive. The dozen or so there, were standing by the open casket at the far end of the room and were comprised of mostly elderly ladies and a few bald-headed men were sitting in the front row, facing them. The lighting was subdued and when one of the ladies moved to the side, I could barely see a form resting in the casket. Seeing this, I openly blurted out several long sobs which caught the attention of everyone up front. Four of the ladies came to the rescue of the receptionist, still patting my hand. When they arrived, the relieved receptionist moved back a few feet to wait until everything was under control. Two ladies sat on either side of me, tenderly holding my hands, and the other two stood in front of me, leaning in with gentle smiles on their faces.

"Poor dear," one would say.

"There, there. You're with friends now," comforted one.

"I don't recognize him, Phyllis. Do you?" said another.

Finally, between my sobs, one of the seated ladies said, "How long have you known Ralph?"

I jerked my head up and turned to her.

"Ralph?" I said clearly and paused for a moment.

"I'm here to see Frank!" I demanded.

My movements and exclamation startled the group and everyone jumped back a little, except for the receptionist. After a few moments of silence and quizzical looks exchanged by all, the receptionist moved back into the circle that had formed around me.

"Oh, dear. I'm so sorry," she said genuinely. "You must be looking for Frank Hastings. He's in the funeral home at the end of the block and around the corner."

Enough strength and composure came back to allow me to rise, apologize for creating such a scene, and thanking them for their kindness. By the time I reached my car, I regained control of my faculties and contemplated driving the extra one hundred yards down the street to the correct chapel for a repeat performance or the thirty miles to my home. As I turned out of the parking lot and headed for the highway, I justified my decision by convincing myself, "It's probably the way Frank and his family would have wanted it."

Rest easy, old friends. I'll miss you.

Membo?

I searched for the prime cell phone reception spot in the middle of a small clearing that was in the center of a dozen old, moss laden mobile homes that appeared to have been tossed by a hurricane under a large oak hammock. Actually, it was my friends hunting camp in southeastern Florida and he and the other twenty members, while talented and devoted hunters, were significantly lacking in community development skills. Although it was an abhorrent clutter of derelict trailers, disabled hunting vehicles, decrepit ladder stands, etc., it was still considered a delightful outdoorsman's retreat inhabited by happy campers most of the weekends during the year. I was always excited to be invited to enjoy the camaraderie of the other hunters. Also, it was an escape from the hectic demands of business life and the responsibilities of my family.

This particular weekend I had been invited to camp but decided to stay home until my wife informed me early Saturday morning that she and her friends just made plans to spend the night at the beach. Upon that announcement, I grabbed my always packed hunting bag, wished her a fun night out with the girls, and headed for camp. Our three kids were all grown and with my twenty-one-year-old son still living at home, I had no worries that everything would fine on the home front.

I had gotten up a little earlier than my host Sunday morning and took that opportunity to go out to the clearing to check my messages. Through the static I could barely hear, I had one, new message from my eldest daughter's phone a little past midnight. Sarah is a first-year resident physician at a large hospital thirty miles from our home and I figured she was working a late shift and called just to say "Hi." But when I heard the somber tone in her voice that simply said, "Dad, this is Sarah. Call me as soon as you get this," I knew that something was very wrong. I searched for a better spot while I hit the call back button.

"Dad . . . it's Mom," she stated plainly. "You need to come home now. She's had a stroke or ruptured brain aneurysm," she continued straight out, knowing I preferred bad news that way. "Dean found her when he got home from work at midnight. She was in bad shape and if he hadn't acted so quickly, we might have lost her."

Tears welled up in my eyes. I swallowed hard and fought to keep composed. Even as Sarah is emotionally tough, I didn't want her to worry about me making the three-hour drive to Tampa.

"They're sending her through all kinds of tests, now." "Laura"—our middle daughter—"is on a flight back from London. She doesn't know, yet," she continued. "We're at Tampa General. Hurry!"

I woke my friend, told him of the bad news, and bolted from camp. The drive across the Florida peninsula is long, flat, and un-distracting. My mind had plenty of time to contemplate events yet to happen and memories from the past.

Cheryl and I had been married almost thirty-two years. Even though the last dozen had contained some rocky stretches, some strewn with boulders, we had stayed together. Mainly as not to disturb our children's upbringing, but also out of stubbornness and maybe fear of the unknown, and maybe, there was something more. We did raise three beautiful kids through it all and the bond between them is awe inspiring. I have to give credit to Cheryl for this, as I was away much of the time addicted to my working world. She was a stay-at-home mom who wove soccer and soft-ball games, piano recitals and cub scouts, complete with a mini-van loaded with car seats, Sippy-cups, puzzle books, old raisins and cheerios stuffed in the corners, and of course the tattered remnants of someone's cherished blankie, all into a tapestry of love. As I drove, my mind raced through the years and brought back vivid memories of Cheryl and the kids . . .

"You need to take your daughter with you!" Cheryl said flatly. "You're gone to conventions and camp so much, Sarah said the other day, 'Is that *man* coming home for dinner tonight?'"

She had me there. Sarah looked up at me from her booster seat, snugged up to the breakfast table, and said with astonished joy, "Me, go with Daddy?" Her wide-eyed look of surprise melted my heart.

"Okay, kid," I said. "Grab your blankie and let's go."

The license bureau is not really high on the list of places to take a three-year-old. Either is the electronic shop or the paint store, but they were on my list of places I had to go that Saturday morning. Her little hands were so fast, getting in to everything in the shops, I had to resort to giving her a plastic finger ring with a big candy jewel on it that my wife had slipped into my pocket before we left, to keep her occupied. And since her mother had dressed her so cutely, in a dark blue dress with white tights, black sandals, and put her hair up in two pig-tails that brushed her face every time she shook her head "No," the shop clerks couldn't resist smiling at her and giving her a little trinket.

Our first two stops finished, I sighed in relief a bit as I waited in line at the license bureau, holding Sarah in my arms. Since the place had nothing to attract her mischievous tiny hands, she was content to be held while playing with her "Radio Shed" refrigerator magnet and colorful paint swatches. She was busy rubbing the half dissolved candy ring on their backs and then sticking them to my shirt when she looked over my shoulder and then back to me.

"He's fancy," she said.

I should have replied, "That's nice, honey," or ignored her altogether. But being under-experienced as I was, I said without thinking, "Who's fancy?"

"He's fancy. Right there!" she said a little louder and pointed her sticky ring finger over my shoulder.

"That's nice, honey," I said. But it was too late. The cat was out of the bag and she was determined to show me her discovery.

"Daddy. Right there!" she demanded my attention and took both her gooey hands, put them on my cheeks and with all her might turned my head to look at her obsession, standing directly behind me.

Not two feet away from us was the biggest, *narliest*, meanest looking biker dude I'd ever seen. My eyes instantly saucered. From his skullcap down to his beat-up engineer boots and all the tattoos, piercings, and ragged clothes in between, he was positively scary-looking.

"See, Daddy. He's fancy," she said, proudly of her find.

Still frozen in my owl-like expression, he said, "Hi, sweetie." Because of his ultra-dark glasses I couldn't be sure if he was speaking to Sarah, or me!

Before I could do anything, Sarah jutted her ring finger at him and said, "Want some?"

"Ahhh!" I screamed inside my head as he leaned forward, opened his mouth to take a bite and stopped an inch shy of the target.

He leaned back, gave a big smile, revealing his large gold tooth with a diamond in it and said in a gravelly voice, "Naw, sweetie. It's all yours." Not to go without giving her new friend something, she peeled the "Misty Mauve" paint swatch from my shirt and plastered it over an obscene patch on his leather vest.

"Good shot, kid," I thought.

He grinned, I turned forward, and that was that. Later, as I fastened Sarah in her car seat, I thought, "Cheryl has to do this every day and take care of our three-month-old, to boot."

The drive to Tampa General continued and so did the replay of our past, in my mind . . .

"Laura! For the last time, sit down!" I yelled while holding a bowl of whipped cream in one hand and shaking a big spoon full of it at her with the other, some of it plopping on the middle of the dinner table.

"Dean! Quit feeding the dog!" I shouted, turning to the other end of the table. "You better not push that off . . . Dean? . . . *Dean!*" and a big glop of pulverized meat loaf splatted on the floor next to his high chair.

"Sarah! Where's your mom!" I said in a strained voice as I took Laura's blankie, tied it around her waist, and then to the back of her chair.

"She's talking on the telephone with Mrs. Kruthers about the my piano recital," she said, oblivious to the surrounding chaos as she fashioned a snowy-white mashed-potato roof and placed it on her green-bean Lincoln-log house.

Totally frustrated at my inability as a dad, I marched in the next room to interrupt my wife's conversation and shouted, "I could use some help in there! Ya know?!"

With the phone in one hand and a calendar in the other, she calmly said, "I just finished," and we walked back in to the kitchen to find the dog eating the meat loaf off the floor, Dean shaking the remaining contents in his Sippy-cup on the dog's head. Sarah was now trying to form a chimney from the potatoes, but without the proper green-bean trusses, it caved in and she started yelling at it. Laura had somehow untied herself and was on all fours on top of the table, shoveling the desert topping in her face with the big spoon. "I wike whip cweam!" she said defiantly.

Cheryl could have turned to me and said sharply, "I leave the room for one minute and this is what happens?" But she didn't. She didn't say anything to me. She just guided the dog outside, gracefully slid Laura back into her chair, and said to Sarah, "Nice house, honey. Now let's see if Sarah-monster can eat it all up." And all was at peace again.

My cell phone rang and startled me as I was driving. It was Sarah checking up on my progress back to Tampa. I told her I was in my hunting "camos" and since Mom was still having tests done, should I stop by the house to change clothes and then go to the hospital. She said no. I'm glad I didn't. I set my cell phone back on the passenger's seat, right next to a little flashlight I had borrowed from my friend so that I could see the padlocks on the gates in the darkness as I was leaving camp. It was a flashlight just like . . .

"Just wike yours, Daddy," Dean said, pointing to the small counter display of colorful miniature flashlights as we entered the auto-repair place.

"What?" I said, paying half attention.

"That one, the wed one!" he continued excitedly. "It's just wike the one in your car." He reached up and grabbed the corner of the display to pull it closer to his gaze. He pulled it a little too far past the edge and it tipped over, spilling its contents on the floor. Annoyed at this, I picked them up and quickly put them back in the display. I snatched the red one from his hand and sternly said, "Dean! Don't touch anything!"

"Great," I thought. "Cheryl had to take the girls to dance class and left me with 'Old Mr. Greentooth.'" I had just christened him with that nickname as the week before he had found one of his sister's hair ties and had a mishap with it. It was a straight piece of a cloth-covered rubber band with a porcelain ball on each end. He put one end in his mouth, clinched his teeth, and stretched out the rubber band with the other ball. Then he let it go. It broke a perfect half-moon shape on the bottom of his two upper baby teeth. To top it off, the next day he found a green child's marking pen and tried to suck the ink out of it. One of the broken teeth absorbed the ink and was forever green.

After thinking a moment, I said, "Okay, Buddy. My car won't be ready for an hour. But if you're real good and don't cause any trouble, I'll buy you that flashlight."

He was an absolute angel. He was so proud and happy to have one just like Daddy's, he put it in the glove box next to mine.

"See, Daddy?" as we pulled in the driveway, "I'm going to keep it next to yours, so I won't lose it."

"What," I said absently, "Oh, sure, sure."

A couple of weeks later I was coerced to watch Mr. Greentooth again. I was working on a project in the garage and decided to keep Dean out of trouble by rolling the windows down in my car and putting him in it with some of his toys. He soon tired of his toys and started playing with the car. He found the electric side mirror switch and began playing with it. I couldn't hear the mirror's tiny electric motors running because of the loud sander I was using. When I realized what he was doing, it was too late. He had burned out the motors in both mirrors.

Furious, I set him down in the passenger's seat and scolded him, "Don't touch anything that's not yours! Understand?!" "Yes," he pouted. No sooner than I turned my attention back to the project, his menacing little hands found the flashlight in the glove box and he began switching it on and off. Seeing that he had gotten into something else sent me over the edge.

I snatched him out of his seat and swatted him on the bottom. "I just told you not to touch anything that wasn't yours!" I yelled.

He slowly raised his head and looked at me through teary eyes as if I were some mistaken, angry god. "But dis is mine," he said in a shaking, tiny voice. "You dot it foe me. Membo?" He reached out with his trembling hand to give me the trophy he earned for his good behavior. I looked at the open glove box and saw my flashlight in its proper place and then to the face of my beautiful son.

I picked him up and hugged him tightly and whispered in his ear, "I'm so sorry, buddy. I do remember."

"I'm so sorry, Dean," I said as I hugged him. "I'm so sorry, I couldn't get here sooner. How's Mom?"

"They're sending her up for her final test now," Dean said calmly. I could see he was exhausted from the ordeal, but my boy was as steady as a rock. Just then a gurney carrying Cheryl rounded the corner of the hallway guided by Sarah on one side and a nurse on the other, headed for the elevator.

"Mom? . . . Mom? . . ., Dad's here," said Sarah.

Cheryl, lying on her side, lifted he head slightly with eyes closed and raised her hand a few inches. "I know," she half smiled. "My head hurts." Our hands touched briefly. The elevator doors closed and I was left staring at the long faces of our frightened children.

The three of us sat in the very large and posh, although empty, waiting room of the Neuro-Surgery unit at Tampa General Hospital. They brought me up to speed on the events of the last ten hours. Cheryl and her friends decided not to go to the beach after all, but went to a local restaurant for appetizers and cocktails. She got home around 11:00 p.m. and went to bed. Dean got home from work around midnight and instead of fixing something to eat and watching TV, he had the strong urge to tell her he was home and goodnight. When she responded incoherently through the locked bedroom door, he broke it down and seeing her condition, called 911 immediately and a one of her neighborhood friends.

I called Laura's cell phone and left a message to call me when she landed in New York. When she called me back, I told her of her mother's condition. She cried the entire flight back to Tampa. When she arrived at the hospital, Cheryl had already been through a very successful surgical procedure to stop the bleeding of her hemorrhaging aneurysm, but not before it caused a stress heart attack. Cheryl's sister flew in from Cincinnati and got there shortly after Laura. We all took overlapping shifts by Cheryl's side in the Neuro ICU for the next twelve days.

That Sunday evening after the surgery, the doctors said she was holding her own, even though the beeping and ticking machines surrounding her were breathing for her and keeping her heart beating. Dean was pale and totally spent, so we all gave him a big hero's hug and sent him home to rest. The girls were hungry and went down to the cafeteria to get something to eat and finally, I was alone with my wife.

I stood at the end of the bed, as the machines crowded both sides. I gently rubbed her feet with my hands as my tears fell on her blanket. I'm not a very religious man, but looking at her and thinking of all the things we'd been through, I was compelled to pray.

"God? I know I haven't talked to you in a very long time, but it's me . . . Dale," I said softly. I paused a moment and then the word sobbed from my lips that seemed to sum up what I was feeling, "Membo?" I stood there for a long time in silent prayer.

As the news of Cheryl's illness spread to friends and family, thousands of prayers were said in her behalf. I can't prove they tipped the scales of fortune in her favor, or not. But she did make a complete and speedy recovery. I truly believe we saw a miracle unveil before us and we are all very grateful for the prayers and good thoughts sent to her.

Our road has become increasingly smoother since then and has led me to realize there are greater forces out there than I thought possible. I've also come to understand that family should come before business and to remember who you're toiling is for. When I get confused on which is the correct path to take in life, I can always set me straight by asking myself, "Membo?"

www.ingramcontent.com/pod-product-compliance
Lightning Source LLC
Chambersburg PA
CBHW030009190526
45157CB00014B/1563